trinitychurchvb.com

All Scripture quotations, unless otherwise indicated, are taken from the Holy Bible, New International Version®, NIV®. Copyright ©1973, 1978, 1984, 2011 by Biblica, Inc.™ Used by permission of Zondervan. All rights reserved worldwide. www.zondervan.com The "NIV" and "New International Version" are trademarks registered in the United States Patent and Trademark Office by Biblica, Inc.™

Copyright © 2024 Trinity Church

All rights reserved.

ISBN: 9798335823173

INTRODUCTION

Theologian, J.I. Packer once wrote, "All roads in the Bible lead to Romans, and all views afforded by the Bible are seen most clearly from Romans, and when the message of Romans gets into a person's heart there is no telling what may happen."

Whether you are exploring Christianity, you are a new follower of Jesus, or you have been a disciple of Jesus for decades, it is our hope that this resource will deepen your understanding of this crucial book of the Bible and ignite in you a passion for living out the gospel that the book of Romans so beautifully conveys.

This 60-day Romans Devotional was written and compiled by the pastoral staff of Trinity Church in 2024, with the desire to combine commentary and devotional thoughts about this letter that has shaped the Christian church since its inception. This devotional is not intended to be exhaustive, as theologians have written commentaries on the book of Romans that are more than 1,000 pages long.

With that in mind, we have divided up the 16 chapters of Romans to be read over a 12-week period based on reading 5 days a week. If you miss a day or a week, no worries, just pick up right where you left off.

Each day's reading contains the following elements:
    A passage from the book of Romans (in the NIV translation)
    A section of commentary on that passage written by a pastor at Trinity Church
    A reflection question or two related to the passage for you to consider
    A prayer prompt

We are thrilled that you have opened this devotional, and it is our prayer that over the next 12 weeks God's Word in the book of Romans will allow you to live in the love of the Father, the salvation of the Son, and the power of the Holy Spirit.

WEEK 1 - DAY 1

Scripture Reading - Romans 1:1-7

[1] Paul, a servant of Christ Jesus, called to be an apostle and set apart for the gospel of God— [2] the gospel he promised beforehand through his prophets in the Holy Scriptures [3] regarding his Son, who as to his earthly life was a descendant of David, [4] and who through the Spirit of holiness was appointed the Son of God in power by his resurrection from the dead: Jesus Christ our Lord. [5] Through him we received grace and apostleship to call all the Gentiles to the obedience that comes from faith for his name's sake. [6] And you also are among those Gentiles who are called to belong to Jesus Christ.

[7] To all in Rome who are loved by God and called to be his holy people: Grace and peace to you from God our Father and from the Lord Jesus Christ.

Commentary:

Paul begins this letter by introducing himself to a group of Christians in Rome that he has heard about but has never met in person. Paul wants to visit the Roman church in person, but he feels compelled to go to Jerusalem first (Acts 19:21), so he writes this letter for the church to read before he comes. Paul introduces himself as a servant of Christ Jesus and then as an apostle that has been set apart. The word "servant" in the text is from the Greek word *doulos* which can also be translated as "bond-servant" or "slave." Paul's identity is first and foremost a bond-servant of Christ - someone who has been redeemed by and belongs to Christ and whose only aim is to obey and serve his master and Lord. Paul also calls himself an apostle, which speaks to his authority to write such a letter to the church in Rome. Paul had been set apart and commissioned by Christ through his encounter with the risen Jesus as recorded in Acts 9.

In this opening paragraph, Paul summarizes the gospel in a nutshell and then spends the rest of the book of Romans unpacking that gospel in more detail. From the outset of his letter, Paul wants to emphasize which gospel (literally "good news") he has been set apart to proclaim. Paul makes it clear that this gospel is the fulfillment of what was spoken about in the Jewish Scriptures and that Jesus is the long-awaited Messiah, descended from King David, fulfilling the covenantal promise that God made in 2 Samuel 7. But Jesus was and is more than "just" the Messiah. Jesus is in fact the Son of God, as proven by his bodily resurrection. The deity of Christ and his physical resurrection are essential elements to the gospel that Paul is going to explain in this letter.

Paul ends his greeting by extending "grace and peace" to the church. Peace (*shalom*) was a common greeting in the Jewish culture, and while Paul still greets the church with peace he also greets them with a word of "grace" (unmerited favor), which is at the core of the Christian gospel. This idea that the gospel offers both grace and peace to all who believe will be a constant thread throughout the remainder of Paul's letter.

Reflection:

Paul introduced himself as a servant and as an apostle. How do you identify yourself as you relate to Christ? Does your identity include both an acknowledgement of your humble position before Jesus and also the high calling he has placed on you?

_____

_____

If someone asked you to summarize "the gospel" what would you say?

_____

_____

Prayer Prompt:

Ask the Lord to use this time in the book of Romans over the next 12 weeks to help deepen your understanding and appreciation of the gospel (the good news).

WEEK 1 - DAY 2

Scripture Reading - Romans 1:8-17

[8] First, I thank my God through Jesus Christ for all of you, because your faith is being reported all over the world. [9] God, whom I serve in my spirit in preaching the gospel of his Son, is my witness how constantly I remember you [10] in my prayers at all times; and I pray that now at last by God's will the way may be opened for me to come to you.

[11] I long to see you so that I may impart to you some spiritual gift to make you strong— [12] that is, that you and I may be mutually encouraged by each other's faith. [13] I do not want you to be unaware, brothers and sisters, that I planned many times to come to you (but have been prevented from doing so until now) in order that I might have a harvest among you, just as I have had among the other Gentiles.

[14] I am obligated both to Greeks and non-Greeks, both to the wise and the foolish. [15] That is why I am so eager to preach the gospel also to you who are in Rome.

[16] For I am not ashamed of the gospel, because it is the power of God that brings salvation to everyone who believes: first to the Jew, then to the Gentile. [17] For in the gospel the righteousness of God is revealed—a righteousness that is by faith from first to last, just as it is written: "The righteous will live by faith."

Commentary:

In this section of his letter to the Romans, Paul continues his introduction and expresses his gratitude for the church in Rome. Paul has heard many reports about the church in Rome from his companions, especially Aquila and Priscilla (Acts 18:1-3, Romans 16:3). Because of the reports of many Jews and Gentiles (non-Jews) coming to accept Christ in Rome, Paul praises God. Taking it one step further, Paul feels compelled to pray for the church in Rome frequently, so much so that Paul says he remembers them in his prayers "at all times." Paul is praying fervently for a group of Christians he has never met, and his prayers have only heightened his desire to come see them in person. Paul also shares in his greeting that he has tried to come to Rome several times before, but he has been prevented from coming so far. Perhaps Paul is referring to Acts 16:6-7 when he tried to enter Bithynia to get on the Egnatian Way which was the primary highway a Roman citizen would take to head to Rome. However, the

Spirit of Jesus wouldn't allow him to enter that region.

Paul ends his introduction in verses 16 and 17 with what many scholars consider to be the theme of the entire letter. Everything that Paul will write in the remainder of his letter can be traced back to these verses. Paul writes that he is not ashamed of the gospel. In spite of the rejection and persecution he has faced since following Jesus, he is not ashamed or afraid to share the good news. Why? Because it is only through this gospel that God grants salvation to all who believe, first for the Jew and then for the Gentile. The church in Rome consisted of both Jews and Gentiles and this first century church was wrestling with how to live and worship in unity in spite of their significant cultural differences. Paul's answer to these difficulties is the gospel. The righteousness (right standing before God) that God offers to all who believe allows both Jews and Gentiles to be welcomed into the new family of God and to come to the same table of worship and fellowship. Paul unpacks how the gospel makes this possible in the pages to come.

Reflection:

How often do you pray for other believers in your life? How does Paul's example of praying for the church in Rome challenge us to pray for other Christians in our lives and around the world?

_____

_____

Paul makes it clear in his introduction that the gospel is for everyone. Why is this significant?

_____

_____

Prayer Prompt:

Ask the Lord to help you to not be ashamed of the gospel and to have the boldness to proclaim it to everyone the Lord places in your path.

WEEK 1 - DAY 3

Scripture Reading - Romans 1:18-23

[18] The wrath of God is being revealed from heaven against all the godlessness and wickedness of people, who suppress the truth by their wickedness, [19] since what may be known about God is plain to them, because God has made it plain to them. [20] For since the creation of the world God's invisible qualities—his eternal power and divine nature—have been clearly seen, being understood from what has been made, so that people are without excuse.

[21] For although they knew God, they neither glorified him as God nor gave thanks to him, but their thinking became futile and their foolish hearts were darkened. [22] Although they claimed to be wise, they became fools [23] and exchanged the glory of the immortal God for images made to look like a mortal human being and birds and animals and reptiles.

Commentary:

These verses begin the first major section in Paul's logical argument for the gospel. In this first portion, running from 1:18 through 3:20, Paul presents the gospel with one clear and fundamental truth - all people have sinned. All people have "missed the mark" in regards to their Creator God and, therefore, all people are worthy of receiving wrath from the Holy God that created them. This is the necessary starting point for Paul, as his readers cannot come to understand and appreciate their need for a savior if they have not realized that they need saving in the first place. In chapter 1, Paul focuses his argument against any person who denies the existence of the one true God. In chapter 2, Paul focuses his argument against any "good person" who believes that their actions have earned their salvation since they are "better" than the godless person.

Paul first addresses those who "suppress the truth" and live godless and wicked lives. These people deny the existence of the one true God. Because of this, they live their lives without considering the idea that a set of rules or standards exists that they'll have to answer to someday. For those who deny the existence of the one true God, Paul's case against them is clear. He writes in 1:20 that creation itself proclaims clearly to all that there is a God who exerted his deity and power when he spoke creation into existence. In Paul's estimation, the evidence of creation is so strong that "all people are without excuse."

Paul goes on to say that because these godless people have rejected God as the Creator, they have instead turned their hearts and minds to "foolish" things and have begun instead worship creation and idols instead of the one true God who created it all. Because of their rejection of God the creator, Paul says they are deserving of the wrath of God. In the rest of chapter 1, we will read what Paul says is the result when a person or a group of people denies the very existence of the creator.

Reflection:

Do you believe that the universe points to the existence of a Creator God? Why or why not?

_____

_____

If a person denies the existence of God, how does that denial impact their morality and purpose in life?

_____

_____

Prayer Prompt:

Give thanks to the Lord for the beauty and order in creation. Ask the Lord to keep you from worshiping creation instead of worshiping the one who created it all.

WEEK 1 - DAY 4

Scripture Reading - Romans 1:24-32

[24] Therefore God gave them over in the sinful desires of their hearts to sexual impurity for the degrading of their bodies with one another. [25] They exchanged the truth about God for a lie, and worshiped and served created things rather than the Creator—who is forever praised. Amen.

[26] Because of this, God gave them over to shameful lusts. Even their women exchanged natural sexual relations for unnatural ones. [27] In the same way the men also abandoned natural relations with women and were inflamed with lust for one another. Men committed shameful acts with other men, and received in themselves the due penalty for their error.

[28] Furthermore, just as they did not think it worthwhile to retain the knowledge of God, so God gave them over to a depraved mind, so that they do what ought not to be done. [29] They have become filled with every kind of wickedness, evil, greed and depravity. They are full of envy, murder, strife, deceit and malice. They are gossips, [30] slanderers, God-haters, insolent, arrogant and boastful; they invent ways of doing evil; they disobey their parents; [31] they have no understanding, no fidelity, no love, no mercy. [32] Although they know God's righteous decree that those who do such things deserve death, they not only continue to do these very things but also approve of those who practice them.

Commentary:

Paul continues following the thread of his logical argument for the gospel in today's reading. In this section, Paul communicates the natural consequences that result when a person denies the existence of God or any moral standard outside themselves. When a person denies the very existence of God, and "exchanges the truth of God for a lie," what types of decisions will this person make? What will become of that person? Paul's language is strong and direct: when a person denies the fundamental truth that God exists, their life will be characterized by actions that contradict what a person "made in the image of God" was meant to be.

Paul describes the behavior of someone who denies God by addressing sins that connect with the very order of creation. If a person denies the truth that creation itself proclaims the existence of God, then they will naturally behave in ways that violate the created order that God instilled in his creation. In the first two chapters of the Bible, it is made clear that when God created the universe, he also established the created order as it relates to gender and to the family unit. In Genesis 1:27 it says, "So God created mankind in his own image, in the image of God he created them; male and female he created them." And in Genesis 2:24 it says, "That is why a man leaves his father and mother and is united to his wife, and they become one flesh." In these verses we see that God's created order sets up the unique and complementary genders of male and female to reflect His image, and that the family order begins with one man and one woman becoming one flesh. If a person denies the existence of a creator, then what would prohibit them from redefining the structure of the family or the delineation of gender? Paul says that this very thing was happening in the first century.

However, sins related to the area of human sexuality are just the tip of the iceberg in Paul's mind. As he moves along in his explanation of a life without the knowledge of God, Paul provides his readers with a laundry list of sins that all stem from the denial of the existence of the one true God. The list can be summarized as actions that reflect the opposite of the character of God, the very being whose image is to be reflected by humanity.

Reflection:

How do you see "the world" redefining and/or restructuring what the creator God established? Why is this "redefining" happening in the world? What is the root of the issue in your opinion?

_____

_____

Prayer Prompt:

Ask the Lord to forgive you for the times that you lived in a way that was opposite of the image of God that you were created to reflect. Consider the list found in 1:29-30 in your prayer.

WEEK 1 - DAY 5

Scripture Reading - Romans 2:1-11

¹ You, therefore, have no excuse, you who pass judgment on someone else, for at whatever point you judge another, you are condemning yourself, because you who pass judgment do the same things. ² Now we know that God's judgment against those who do such things is based on truth. ³ So when you, a mere human being, pass judgment on them and yet do the same things, do you think you will escape God's judgment? ⁴ Or do you show contempt for the riches of his kindness, forbearance and patience, not realizing that God's kindness is intended to lead you to repentance?

⁵ But because of your stubbornness and your unrepentant heart, you are storing up wrath against yourself for the day of God's wrath, when his righteous judgment will be revealed. ⁶ God "will repay each person according to what they have done." ⁷ To those who by persistence in doing good seek glory, honor and immortality, he will give eternal life. ⁸ But for those who are self-seeking and who reject the truth and follow evil, there will be wrath and anger. ⁹ There will be trouble and distress for every human being who does evil: first for the Jew, then for the Gentile; ¹⁰ but glory, honor and peace for everyone who does good: first for the Jew, then for the Gentile. ¹¹ For God does not show favoritism.

Commentary:

After making clear in the previous chapter that those who deny the existence of God are deserving of the wrath of God, Paul shifts his argument to a different audience. Paul can imagine that a number of people would be reading through his previous paragraph and saying to themselves, "Well, those people certainly deserve God's judgment, but I'm much better than those people." Paul knows that some readers might look at the list of sins in chapter 1 and conclude that those godless people deserve judgment and condemnation. Paul challenges this second group by saying, "You, therefore, have no excuse, you who pass judgment on someone else, for at whatever point you judge another, you are condemning yourself, because you who pass judgment do the same things."

Just as those who denied the existence of God were "without excuse" because of creation's clear proclamation that God exists, those who believe they are a "good person" are also without excuse. Paul's argument here is that all people, whether they admit to the existence of God or not, have an innate understanding of right and wrong. Because of this understanding, a person is able to look at the actions of another and deem those actions as either right or wrong. With this moral conscience that they possess, humans pass judgment on the actions of others. Paul is making the argument that every human at some point in their life has violated their own conscience. Every human at one time or another has done something that went against what they internally knew to be right. A person chose to be selfish when they knew they should be generous. A person lied when they knew that it was right to tell the truth. The list is endless. Paul presents the idea that even if you don't think you are "as bad" as the people he described in the first chapter, everyone is still guilty. All people have violated the law put in place by the creator God, and all have fallen short of that standard as evidenced by their own conscience. This means that even the "good" person is still deserving of the wrath of God and in need of salvation.

Reflection:

Do you find yourself using those around you as the measuring stick for your "goodness"? What is the problem with using other people as the standard by which you measure yourself?

_____

_____

Can you think of a time this week that you did something that went against what you knew to be right? What does that mean we are worthy of according to Paul in this section?

_____

_____

Prayer Prompt:

Ask the Lord to expose within you the tendency we have as humans to compare ourselves to others instead of to the standard of God himself. Repent of those times this week you have fallen short of the standard God has set.

WEEK 2 - DAY 1

Scripture Reading - Romans 2:12-16

¹² All who sin apart from the law will also perish apart from the law, and all who sin under the law will be judged by the law. ¹³ For it is not those who hear the law who are righteous in God's sight, but it is those who obey the law who will be declared righteous. ¹⁴ (Indeed, when Gentiles, who do not have the law, do by nature things required by the law, they are a law for themselves, even though they do not have the law. ¹⁵ They show that the requirements of the law are written on their hearts, their consciences also bearing witness, and their thoughts sometimes accusing them and at other times even defending them.) ¹⁶ This will take place on the day when God judges people's secrets through Jesus Christ, as my gospel declares.

Commentary:

When we see in the news that a terrible tragedy has happened, such as a mass shooting or an act of terror, there is something in us, in everyone, that says, "That is wrong!" We innately recognize that something has happened that should not have happened. An instinct in us tells us that people should not murder other people, just like it tells us people should not lie or steal. But this is not a new phenomenon. If you consider cultures throughout history, there seems to be a set of rights and wrongs that transcend across all cultures.

How can this be? Paul says this is because each person has "the requirements of the law written on their hearts" (Romans 2:15). This is what some have called the natural law. As C.S. Lewis put it, the natural law is a set of laws "which none of us made, but which we find pressing on us."[1] Paul uses this fact here to prove that "God does not show favoritism" (Romans 2:11). Was God unfair in giving the written law to Israel but not to others? Paul's answer is no because all people have a law whether written on stone tablets or on their hearts. Not only do all people have a law, but just as Israel failed to follow the law they were given, so too has the rest of the world failed to follow the law on their hearts. Therefore, God is just and impartial to judge all according to the law which they received (Romans 2:13).

Reflection:

In this passage, Paul talks about the difference between hearing the Law and obeying the Law. How have you seen that difference play out in your life?

_____

_____

What emotion do you feel when you reflect on the truth that God is an impartial judge? Why?

_____

_____

Prayer Prompt:

Take a moment to thank God for his impartial justice and the fact that, because of the grace given to us in Christ, we have nothing to fear when we stand before him on the day of judgment.

WEEK 2 - DAY 2

Scripture Reading - Romans 2:17-24

[17] Now you, if you call yourself a Jew; if you rely on the law and boast in God; [18] if you know his will and approve of what is superior because you are instructed by the law; [19] if you are convinced that you are a guide for the blind, a light for those who are in the dark, [20] an instructor of the foolish, a teacher of little children, because you have in the law the embodiment of knowledge and truth— [21] you, then, who teach others, do you not teach yourself? You who preach against stealing, do you steal? [22] You who say that people should not commit adultery, do you commit adultery? You who abhor idols, do you rob temples? [23] You who boast in the law, do you dishonor God by breaking the law? [24] As it is written: "God's name is blasphemed among the Gentiles because of you."

Commentary:

No one likes a hypocrite. When we see someone saying one thing but doing something else, frustration rises up inside us. The Apostle Paul felt this frustration toward some of the people he was writing to in Rome. In the verses prior to this passage, Paul established that God was not showing partiality in giving the Jewish people the law and that mere possession of the law is not an advantage. However, for many of the Jews in Paul's day, being the ones to whom God gave the law had become a source of pride and status. There was a problem though. They were hypocrites. These people took pride in possessing the law and even considered themselves guides and teachers "of the foolish" (Romans 2:20), yet they did not practice the law in their own lives. They were quick to point out the flaws in the lives of those around them but they were blind to the issues in their own lives.

Paul's words echo what Jesus said in the Sermon on the Mount, "Why do you look at the speck of sawdust in your brother's eye and pay no attention to the plank in your own eye?...You hypocrite, first take the plank out of your own eye, and then you will see clearly to remove the speck from your brother's eye" (Matthew 7:3-5). Hypocrisy results in pain and brokenness, but living in line with what we claim to believe brings healing and wholeness.

Paul wants his readers to not only be aware of their hypocrisy, but he also wants to remind them of the devastating consequences of hypocrisy. First, in teaching but not doing, they are actually dishonoring the very one who gave them the law in the first place. They may "boast in God" (Romans 2:17) but their lives prove they do not love God. Second, God's design was for the faithful lives of his people to point others back to his goodness and his holiness which would draw non-believers to himself. Hypocrisy does the opposite- it gives people a false idea of who God is and drives people away from him.

Reflection:

When is a time when someone in your life acted hypocritically? How did you feel when they acted this way?

_____

_____

What steps can you take to live out God's Word rather than just know it?

_____

_____

Prayer Prompt:

Ask God to reveal any areas in your life where you have been a hypocrite. If the Lord brings anything to mind, take a moment to repent and ask God to help you live more in line with his Word.

WEEK 2 - DAY 3

Scripture Reading - Romans 2:25-29

^{25} Circumcision has value if you observe the law, but if you break the law, you have become as though you had not been circumcised. ^{26} So then, if those who are not circumcised keep the law's requirements, will they not be regarded as though they were circumcised? ^{27} The one who is not circumcised physically and yet obeys the law will condemn you who, even though you have the written code and circumcision, are a lawbreaker.

^{28} A person is not a Jew who is one only outwardly, nor is circumcision merely outward and physical. ^{29} No, a person is a Jew who is one inwardly; and circumcision is circumcision of the heart, by the Spirit, not by the written code. Such a person's praise is not from other people, but from God.

Commentary:

In the Old Testament, circumcision was the symbol of the covenant between God and the people of Israel. It was a symbol to identify who was a member of the people of God and who was not. They believed that just having the symbol of circumcision would save them, but Paul wanted them to know that the symbol only had value if it had substance. The outward mark must be accompanied by the inward reality of a heart that has been changed by the Holy Spirit. A changed heart leads to a changed life ("observe the law"). Paul will discuss this in more detail in Romans 9-11.

Today, we go to church, read the Bible and take communion, which are all good things that believers should be doing, but none of these things save us. We can go to church and not worship. We can read the Bible and not know God. We can take communion and not consider the weight and beauty of what it symbolizes. This is what theologian and pastor Tim Keller called dead orthodoxy. Dead orthodoxy is when we say the right words and do the right actions but there is no real change in our hearts. We do Christian things but our lives remain unaffected. Paul says that rather than circumcision, rather than dead orthodoxy, we need a "circumcision of the heart, by the Spirit" (Romans 2:29). When we truly repent and turn to Jesus, the Holy Spirit works in us to transform us from the inside out. Works, therefore, do not save us but become a joyful overflow of a heart changed by "faith working through love" (Galatians 5:6).

Reflection:

How can you keep worshiping at church, reading your Bible, and taking communion as meaningful times with God rather than simply becoming "dead orthodoxy"?

_____

_____

In your Christian walk, do you find that you are more often doing "Christian things" for God or out of a love from God?

_____

_____

Prayer Prompt:

Thank God for the fact that he does not leave us in dead orthodoxy but works in our hearts to draw us closer to himself and into his mission to save the world through Jesus.

WEEK 2 - DAY 4

Scripture Reading - Romans 3:1-8

[1] What advantage, then, is there in being a Jew, or what value is there in circumcision? [2] Much in every way! First of all, the Jews have been entrusted with the very words of God. [3] What if some were unfaithful? Will their unfaithfulness nullify God's faithfulness? [4] Not at all! Let God be true, and every human being a liar. As it is written:

"So that you may be proved right when you speak
 and prevail when you judge."

[5] But if our unrighteousness brings out God's righteousness more clearly, what shall we say? That God is unjust in bringing his wrath on us? (I am using a human argument.) [6] Certainly not! If that were so, how could God judge the world? [7] Someone might argue, "If my falsehood enhances God's truthfulness and so increases his glory, why am I still condemned as a sinner?" [8] Why not say—as some slanderously claim that we say—"Let us do evil that good may result"? Their condemnation is just!

Commentary:

In chapter 2, Paul argued that both Jews and Gentiles are under God's judgment and are in need of "circumcision of the heart, by the Spirit" (Romans 2:29). Paul anticipates that this conclusion will leave his readers with some questions which he seeks to preemptively answer.

Q1: Is there any advantage to being a Jew?
A1: Of course! It is a huge blessing to be the ones to whom God entrusted his Word.

Q2: But many of the Jews failed to believe in Jesus. Did God fail to keep his Word and promises to them?
A2: Absolutely not! God always promised judgment for Israel if they rejected him. Not only is God keeping his promise to judge Israel, but he also kept his promise, through the faith of the Gentiles, to advance his mission to save the whole world.

Q3: Well then, if our failures and sins advance God's mission and show his righteousness and glory, then is he unjust to punish us?
A3: No! If that were true then God would not be able to judge anyone. God is good enough to take human failure and sin and work it for the

good of his purposes, but this does not mean we should not care about our sin. Otherwise, some might even try to say they should sin more so that God's righteousness and glory would be even more obvious. Those who hold this mindset misunderstand God's righteousness and the gospel and "their condemnation is just."

Reflection:

What are two ways that you have seen God use your failures to bring about his glory?

_____

_____

_____

Prayer Prompt:

Thank God for his faithfulness in your life. Thank him that he is so good that you cannot "out sin" his grace but that he continually draws you back to himself.

WEEK 2 - DAY 5

Scripture Reading - Romans 3:9-20

⁹ What shall we conclude then? Do we have any advantage? Not at all! For we have already made the charge that Jews and Gentiles alike are all under the power of sin. ¹⁰ As it is written:

"There is no one righteous, not even one;
¹¹   there is no one who understands;
   there is no one who seeks God.
¹² All have turned away,
   they have together become worthless;
there is no one who does good,
   not even one."
¹³ "Their throats are open graves;
   their tongues practice deceit."
"The poison of vipers is on their lips."
¹⁴   "Their mouths are full of cursing and bitterness."
¹⁵ "Their feet are swift to shed blood;
¹⁶   ruin and misery mark their ways,
¹⁷ and the way of peace they do not know."
¹⁸   "There is no fear of God before their eyes."

¹⁹ Now we know that whatever the law says, it says to those who are under the law, so that every mouth may be silenced and the whole world held accountable to God. ²⁰ Therefore no one will be declared righteous in God's sight by the works of the law; rather, through the law we become conscious of our sin.

Commentary:

Are humans basically good or bad? This is a question that has been asked for centuries. Biblically, the answer is that humans are both. When God created, he looked at all that he had made and declared that it was good. This includes humanity, which has the even greater honor of being made in the image of God. However, while created good, sin entered the world through the disobedience of Adam and Eve and left all humanity- past, present, and future-"under the power of sin" (3:9). The impact of this is so deep that our sin nature is present even in the earliest moments of life in the womb (Psalm 51:5).

In the passage, Paul brings to a close his first major section of his letter that began back in 1:18. He drives home the point that because of sin, "there is no one righteous, not even one" (3:10). Paul's prognosis may seem bleak, and many today, including many in the church, want to reject the idea that humanity is broken and sinful, and instead want to believe that we are good. However, the reality is that there is freedom in Paul's words. If someone has pain in their abdomen, and ignores it, they could be ignoring something that will get worse or even kill them. However, if they go to the doctor, the problem can be discovered, treated, and full health can be restored. This is Paul's point. "Works of the law" (3:19) cannot save anyone but, as Paul writes, "through the law we become conscious of our sin" (3:20). God has graciously given humanity the natural law written on our hearts and his revealed law in his Word so that we can become conscious of the disease of sin that is ravaging our lives. Once we acknowledge our sin, we are then able to go to Jesus, the good physician (Mark 2:17), who is able to heal and restore us to God's good design. A person will only seek out a savior once they realize that they are in need of saving.

Reflection:

How have you seen the brokenness of sin impact your life?

_____

_____

Is there any sin in your life that you need to acknowledge and bring it before God so that he can heal you?

_____

_____

Prayer Prompt:

Take a moment to acknowledge and repent of your sin before God knowing that "if we confess our sins, he is faithful and just to forgive us our sins and purify us from all unrighteousness" (1 John 1:9).

WEEK 3 - DAY 1

Scripture Reading - Romans 3:21-26

[21] But now apart from the law the righteousness of God has been made known, to which the Law and the Prophets testify. [22] This righteousness is given through faith in Jesus Christ to all who believe. There is no difference between Jew and Gentile, [23] for all have sinned and fall short of the glory of God, [24] and all are justified freely by his grace through the redemption that came by Christ Jesus. [25] God presented Christ as a sacrifice of atonement, through the shedding of his blood—to be received by faith. He did this to demonstrate his righteousness, because in his forbearance he had left the sins committed beforehand unpunished— [26] he did it to demonstrate his righteousness at the present time, so as to be just and the one who justifies those who have faith in Jesus.

Commentary:

If the book of Romans ended at chapter 3 verse 20, it would be a pretty depressing book. However, with the phrase "But now," Paul turns the page in his argument to the "good news." After establishing the fact that all have sinned, Paul spends the next two chapters explaining how sinners can be declared righteous by God in spite of their sin. In verse 21, when Paul writes "But now," he changes the topic from the previous verses (3:9-20) that focus on how no one is declared righteous by their works. In doing so, Paul points us back to the theme of 1:17, how the gospel reveals God's righteousness. Paul also mentions that the whole Old Testament, which he calls "the Law and the Prophets," has pointed to this very concept. This shows us that the heart of the gospel is not just a New Testament idea. God's ultimate rescue plan for sinful humans, the gospel, has been woven throughout all of Scripture.

Verses 22-25 are a great four-verse summary of the gospel. These verses answer the questions: How can we become righteous? Through faith in Jesus. Who is eligible for becoming righteous? All who believe. Why do we need righteousness? Because all have sinned and fall short of the glory of God. How are we made righteous? All are justified freely through God's grace. How exactly was our redemption purchased? God presented Jesus as a sacrifice of atonement.

In a world where many believe the message of the Bible is, "do good works in order to be saved," Romans 3:22-25 refreshingly reminds us that true salvation is a gift from God.

Reflection:

Why do you think so many in our world believe salvation comes through doing good works?

_____

_____

How does it feel to read today's verses after spending the last two weeks focusing on our sin?

_____

_____

Prayer Prompt:

Thank God for the opportunity to be declared righteous through the blood of Christ. And, thank him for the gift of eternal life, through his Son's work on the cross. It's important for Christians to remember that, although salvation is a gift, it was purchased at a tremendous price.

WEEK 3 - DAY 2

Scripture Reading - Romans 3:27-31

[27] Where, then, is boasting? It is excluded. Because of what law? The law that requires works? No, because of the law that requires faith. [28] For we maintain that a person is justified by faith apart from the works of the law. [29] Or is God the God of Jews only? Is he not the God of Gentiles too? Yes, of Gentiles too, [30] since there is only one God, who will justify the circumcised by faith and the uncircumcised through that same faith. [31] Do we, then, nullify the law by this faith? Not at all! Rather, we uphold the law.

Commentary:

In the last three chapters, Paul has slowly developed this argument: Through the law, God's righteousness has been made known, and both Jews and Gentiles have this law, whether written on paper or on their hearts. However, no one has lived up to the law that was given to them. Therefore, all are condemned under the law, but, thanks to Jesus taking on our condemnation, all can be forgiven and restored to God.

Now, in this passage, Paul addresses Jews in Rome who viewed possessing the written law as a point of pride, as something they could boast about. The law demanded works, and if someone could have successfully done them all then they could have been declared righteous on the basis of those works. They would have a reason to boast in their own accomplishment. The problem is that, since the fall, sin has rendered righteousness by works impossible. The good news is that we are not left without hope. Jesus, the eternal Son of God, came to earth, took on humanity, and lived a perfect life. He fulfilled the law. What was impossible for mere humanity was accomplished by Jesus. "For nothing will be impossible with God" (Luke 1:37 ESV).

Jesus's perfect life did not change the fact that we are condemned by the law, but, in his death and resurrection, we have hope as we put our faith in Jesus. We accept his righteousness in place of our unrighteousness. And now, since our hope is in the work of Jesus rather than our own works, we have no ability to boast. As Paul says, "[boasting] is excluded." As humans, our default is to work hard to earn our salvation, however, all people, Jew and the Gentile, male and female, have one proper response to our need for salvation. We are to gladly admit our weakness and place our faith in Jesus "since there is only one God, who will justify…through that same faith."

Reflection:

What are things that you are tempted to boast in rather than boasting in Christ?

_____

_____

How does it change your day-to-day life knowing that Jesus accomplished the work for you?

_____

_____

Prayer Prompt:

Take a moment to praise God that when we could not save ourselves. When we were dying under the law, he sent his one and only Son to save us by doing what we could not.

WEEK 3 - DAY 3

Scripture Reading - Romans 4:1-8

¹ What then shall we say that Abraham, our forefather according to the flesh, discovered in this matter? ² If, in fact, Abraham was justified by works, he had something to boast about—but not before God. ³ What does Scripture say? "Abraham believed God, and it was credited to him as righteousness."

⁴ Now to the one who works, wages are not credited as a gift but as an obligation. ⁵ However, to the one who does not work but trusts God who justifies the ungodly, their faith is credited as righteousness. ⁶ David says the same thing when he speaks of the blessedness of the one to whom God credits righteousness apart from works:

> ⁷ "Blessed are those
> whose transgressions are forgiven,
> whose sins are covered.
> ⁸ Blessed is the one
> whose sin the Lord will never count against them."

Commentary:

In this chapter, Paul continues to make the case that salvation has always come through faith alone and not by works. To make this case, he turns to one of the most important figures in all of the Old Testament, Abraham. In the Book of Genesis, we find that Abraham lived in his father's household in Herron (modern-day Turkey), whose people worshiped many gods. But then one day, God came to Abraham and told him to leave his country and his people and worship him alone (Genesis 12). Abraham obeyed God. He gathered his belongings, his sheep, his cattle, his tents and then, along with his wife and some of his relatives, he left Herron. Where did he go? God led him to the southwest, to the Land of Canaan, where the nation of Israel would eventually be located. When Abraham arrived, God told him that the land would belong to his descendants and that they would be a great nation.

In Romans 4:3, Paul quotes Genesis 15:6, "Abram believed the LORD, and he credited it to him as righteousness." Paul was pointing out that despite Abraham's great acts of obedience, those acts were not what "saved" him from God's wrath. What saved Abraham was his faith in the one true God. Abraham both believed and trusted in God. Remarkably, God accepts (considers righteous) unholy people based upon nothing but their faith. Biblical scholar F.F. Bruce wrote that God, who alone does great wonders, created the universe from nothing, calls the dead to life, and justifies the ungodly- "the greatest of all his wonders."[1] Paul wanted his readers to know that just as Abraham was saved through faith, they, and we today, are saved in that same way- through faith alone that is placed in God as revealed in Jesus.

Reflection:

Abraham was asked to, in faith, leave his family, his people, and his country. What is something God has asked you to do in faith in the past?

_____

_____

What is something that you believe God is asking you to do in faith today?

_____

_____

Prayer Prompt:

Take time to thank the Lord that you are saved through faith alone and ask the Lord to give you the strength to be obedient to his call and to walk in faith today.

WEEK 3 - DAY 4

Scripture Reading - Romans 4:9-17

⁹ Is this blessedness only for the circumcised, or also for the uncircumcised? We have been saying that Abraham's faith was credited to him as righteousness. ¹⁰ Under what circumstances was it credited? Was it after he was circumcised, or before? It was not after, but before! ¹¹ And he received circumcision as a sign, a seal of the righteousness that he had by faith while he was still uncircumcised. So then, he is the father of all who believe but have not been circumcised, in order that righteousness might be credited to them. ¹² And he is then also the father of the circumcised who not only are circumcised but who also follow in the footsteps of the faith that our father Abraham had before he was circumcised.

¹³ It was not through the law that Abraham and his offspring received the promise that he would be heir of the world, but through the righteousness that comes by faith. ¹⁴ For if those who depend on the law are heirs, faith means nothing and the promise is worthless, ¹⁵ because the law brings wrath. And where there is no law there is no transgression.

¹⁶ Therefore, the promise comes by faith, so that it may be by grace and may be guaranteed to all Abraham's offspring—not only to those who are of the law but also to those who have the faith of Abraham. He is the father of us all. ¹⁷ As it is written: "I have made you a father of many nations." He is our father in the sight of God, in whom he believed—the God who gives life to the dead and calls into being things that were not.

Commentary:

In this section Paul continues his argument for salvation through grace and not obedience to the law. Verse 16 stresses that all are saved by grace, both Jew and Gentile. One of the best illustrations of grace in literature is in Victor Hugo's 1862 novel, Les Misérables. In the novel, Jean Valjean is at the end of his rope. After serving nineteen years of hard labor—for stealing a loaf of bread to feed his nephew—he finds himself on parole. But he is in real danger of being thrown back into prison. One night, in utter desperation, he knocks on a random church door and he meets Bishop Myriel.

Jean Valjean says, "I am on parole. I need food." When the Bishop tells him to come inside, Jean Valjean replies, "No. You don't want me inside. I'm a convict. Look at my passport. It says I am very dangerous." But the Bishop says he doesn't care. He tells Jean Valjean to come in, and eat and sleep.

Reluctantly, Jean Valjean enters the dimly lit church. He is thankful for the food and the bed, and he promises the bishop that he will become a new man. But, desperate for money, in the night Jean Valjean gets up and maneuvers through the church—taking what silver items he can carry. The bishop is awakened by the noise. When he gets up to investigate, Jean Valjean jumps out of the shadows and violently strikes the bishop—knocking him to the ground. After this, Jean Valjean disappears into the night, silver in tow.

The next day, soldiers come to the church, and with them they have a prisoner. It's Jean Valjean. The captain of the soldiers tells the Bishop, "We found this man with your silver. He claims that you gave it to him." Shockingly, Bishop Myriel replies, "Yes! Yes, I have given it to him, the silver is his." After the soldiers leave, the bishop insists that Jean Valjean keep the silver, and for good measure the bishop even tosses in the church's silver candlestick holders. Jean Valjean is understandably stunned. What he has experienced is grace, an undeserved favor. Grace is what Jesus offers all who come to him, repent, and believe in him.

Reflection:

When is a time when you were guilty of something, but you ended up being let "off the hook?" How does your receiving of God's grace impact your willingness to extend grace to others?

_____

_____

Prayer Prompt:

Give thanks to the Lord that he has extended to us unimaginable grace.

WEEK 3 - DAY 5

Scripture Reading - Romans 4:18-25

[18] Against all hope, Abraham in hope believed and so became the father of many nations, just as it had been said to him, "So shall your offspring be." [19] Without weakening in his faith, he faced the fact that his body was as good as dead—since he was about a hundred years old—and that Sarah's womb was also dead. [20] Yet he did not waver through unbelief regarding the promise of God, but was strengthened in his faith and gave glory to God, [21] being fully persuaded that God had power to do what he had promised. [22] This is why "it was credited to him as righteousness." [23] The words "it was credited to him" were written not for him alone, [24] but also for us, to whom God will credit righteousness—for us who believe in him who raised Jesus our Lord from the dead. [25] He was delivered over to death for our sins and was raised to life for our justification.

Commentary:

In Genesis, God made a massive promise to Abraham. He said, "I will make you into a great nation, and I will bless you...and all peoples on earth will be blessed through you" (Genesis 12:1-3). Abraham believed God, but years passed and Abraham had no children. In those days, you could not become a great nation without a large family. However, even though Abraham was nearly a hundred years old and his wife, Sarah, could no longer have kids, he "was strengthened in his faith and gave glory to God, being fully persuaded that God had the power to do what he promised." There was no natural way for the promise of God to be fulfilled, but Abraham's faith grew because he knew his God was able to do the supernatural.

The faith of Abraham is presented by Paul as a core example that all who believe in God are to follow. It is this faith that brings us into relationship with God as Genesis says, "Abraham believed the Lord, and he credited it to him as righteousness" (Genesis 15:6). Paul says that these words were not written just for Abraham, because this faith that leads to righteousness was not for Abraham only, "but also for us, to whom God will credit righteousness – for us who believe in him who raised Jesus our Lord from the dead."

We can hold fast to faith, and even grow in our faith, in the midst of hard situations because we know that our God is able. He was able to give Abraham and Sarah their son Issac, he was able to split the Red

Sea, he was able to raise Jesus from the dead, and he is able to bring life and hope to the places that you feel are lost. God is working when we don't see it, and even now we can be strengthened in our faith and give glory to God.

Reflection:

When is a time that something seemed impossible but you saw God accomplish it?

_____

_____

What is an area of your life that you need to step out in faith and believe that "God has the power to do what he promised"?

_____

_____

Prayer Prompt:

Take a moment to thank God for giving you situations that seem impossible so that you can rely on him and grow in your faith and joy.

WEEK 4 - DAY 1

Scripture Reading - Romans 5:1-5

[1] Therefore, since we have been justified through faith, we have peace with God through our Lord Jesus Christ, [2] through whom we have gained access by faith into this grace in which we now stand. And we boast in the hope of the glory of God. [3] Not only so, but we also glory in our sufferings, because we know that suffering produces perseverance; [4] perseverance, character; and character, hope. [5] And hope does not put us to shame, because God's love has been poured out into our hearts through the Holy Spirit, who has been given to us.

Commentary:

Paul begins this chapter by revealing to us the many blessings we receive through being justified (declared righteous) by faith in Christ. It is because of Christ that we now have peace with God, access to His grace, hope in the midst of our sufferings, and the love of God which is being poured into us through the Holy Spirit.

Throughout the history of the world, our relationship with God has been anything but peaceful. From the moment Adam and Eve disobeyed God in the Garden of Eden, all of us have been fighting against God because of our sin. But thanks be to God, we do not have to stay stuck in that life of conflict because we have peace with God because of his Son, Jesus Christ. He has reconciled us to God (Colossians 1:22).

Paul also points us to the hope that comes as the result of our justification through faith. Because of our salvation in Christ, we are given assurance that one day we will share in God's glory. And because of this assurance we have hope, hope that gives us the ability to also glory in our sufferings. For we know that in our suffering, God will use it to work towards building our perseverance, character, and hope.

As we go through this life, we need to remember that what we experience in it is only temporary in comparison with the eternal life that awaits us with God. The hope that we have received is not rooted in anything that we have done, but rather, what has been done by Christ and gifted to us.

Reflection:

What does it mean to have peace with God? What are the implications of this reality for us?

_____

_____

What good things can result as we endure suffering? How have you experienced this?

_____

_____

Prayer Prompt:

Take a moment to thank God that despite the things we may face in this life, he gives us the ability to hope and stand firm on his promises.

WEEK 4 - DAY 2

Scripture Reading - Romans 5:6-11

[6] You see, at just the right time, when we were still powerless, Christ died for the ungodly. [7] Very rarely will anyone die for a righteous person, though for a good person someone might possibly dare to die. [8] But God demonstrates his own love for us in this: While we were still sinners, Christ died for us. [9] Since we have now been justified by his blood, how much more shall we be saved from God's wrath through him! [10] For if, while we were God's enemies, we were reconciled to him through the death of his Son, how much more, having been reconciled, shall we be saved through his life! [11] Not only is this so, but we also boast in God through our Lord Jesus Christ, through whom we have now received reconciliation.

Commentary:

While we were still dead in our sin, and still totally unworthy, Christ came and rescued us so that we could be free! Paul declares that it is by faith that we are justified, not through anything we could have done, for our justification only comes by faith in his son, Jesus Christ. To further make the point that salvation is not through works, Paul emphasizes that Jesus was willing to die for us while we were as far from him as we could ever be.

The peace we now have with God comes only through the undeserved love and grace God gives to us through the death of Jesus.

As believers, we will escape God's wrath, not because we are worthy, but because we have been saved by his grace. This truth concerning God's grace allows us to experience a joy that can only come from being in a right relationship with God. The word "reconciled" means that we have been brought back into fellowship with God. Paul explains that since mankind declared war on God through sin, they deserved to be condemned eternally. But God did not declare war on us, instead, he sent his Son, so that we might be reconciled to God.

Reflection:

How has God demonstrated his love for us?

_____

_____

What does being reconciled to God mean for your future here on Earth? What does being reconciled to God mean for your eternal future?

_____

_____

Prayer Prompt:

Take a moment to reflect on your life before you knew Christ. Spend time in prayer thanking God that despite your sin, he came to rescue you. Thank him for the gift of your salvation.

WEEK 4 - DAY 3

Scripture Reading - Romans 5:12-17

[12] Therefore, just as sin entered the world through one man, and death through sin, and in this way death came to all people, because all sinned. [13] To be sure, sin was in the world before the law was given, but sin is not charged against anyone's account where there is no law. [14] Nevertheless, death reigned from the time of Adam to the time of Moses, even over those who did not sin by breaking a command, as did Adam, who is a pattern of the one to come. [15] But the gift is not like the trespass. For if the many died by the trespass of the one man, how much more did God's grace and the gift that came by the grace of the one man, Jesus Christ, overflow to the many! [16] Nor can the gift of God be compared with the result of one man's sin: The judgment followed one sin and brought condemnation, but the gift followed many trespasses and brought justification. [17] For if, by the trespass of the one man, death reigned through that one man, how much more will those who receive God's abundant provision of grace and of the gift of righteousness reign in life through the one man, Jesus Christ.

Commentary:

After discussing the reconciliation of believers to God through his son, Paul now talks about the certainty of salvation. He shows us the difference between the actions of Adam in the Garden of Eden and of Christ. In these verses, Paul highlights the power of Jesus as the one who came to undo the consequences of sin to ensure that those who are in him will have eternal life.

Unlike Adam, who chose not to obey God and who brought death as a result of sin, Paul says that it is Christ who brings life as a result of his sacrificial death. Therefore, all who belong to Christ can now be confident that they are under his grace and have been freed from the curse and death that Adam unleashed on mankind. Paul teaches this same truth in 1 Corinthians 15:21-22 when he writes, "For since death came through a man, the resurrection of the dead comes also through a man. For as in Adam all die, so in Christ all will be made alive."

To reiterate that both Jews and Gentiles are equally in need of a Savior, Paul goes all the way back to Adam, the first human, as the one who introduced universal sin and death. Therefore all descendants of Adam (both Jews and Gentiles) are in need of the same Savior. As a result of our fallen nature we deserved death, but through Christ, we are promised the new gift of life and are welcomed into the family of God on equal footing for all eternity. Because of Adam's disobedience, death reigned, but in Jesus Christ we have been delivered from death and given new life.

Reflection:

Compare and contrast Adam and Jesus. How are they similar? How are they different?

_____

_____

What is God's solution to the problem of sin and death that came through Adam's sin?

_____

_____

Prayer Prompt:

Take a moment to thank God that in him, we have received his grace. Thank him for the free gift of righteousness that now reigns in your life as a result of your faith in Jesus.

WEEK 4 - DAY 4

Scripture Reading - Romans 5:18-21

[18] Consequently, just as one trespass resulted in condemnation for all people, so also one righteous act resulted in justification and life for all people. [19] For just as through the disobedience of the one man the many were made sinners, so also through the obedience of the one man the many will be made righteous. [20] The law was brought in so that the trespass might increase. But where sin increased, grace increased all the more, [21] so that, just as sin reigned in death, so also grace might reign through righteousness to bring eternal life through Jesus Christ our Lord.

Commentary:

These last four verses in Romans 5 bring us to the conclusion of a massive section on justification by faith alone that Paul began back in 3:21. As a reminder, justification is, very simply, when God declares the guilty sinner to be righteous (in right standing with God). He does not make us perfect in our present day-to-day lives – we continue to sin, which Paul will address more in the next chapter. But God does declare us to be righteous, such that our status is dramatically changed. We go from being condemned to being justified. Even though we were deserving of death and God's wrath, God has declared all who believe in him righteous.

In these verses, Paul continues to contrast "the trespass of one" found in Adam to "the obedience of one", found in the finished work of Christ on the cross. It was the sin of Adam that brought sin and death to all. But through the obedience of Christ and his sacrifice, life and freedom from sin's power has been made available to all. Because of this, we've been given a new life, a life we now are now called to live in obedience to God.

Paul concludes this section with a final discussion of the law and grace. Grace was not an addition to God's plan, but rather, it was part of God's plan from the beginning. God gave the law through Moses not to replace his grace, but to reveal our need for grace. The law was temporary, but His grace is eternal. Though we still battle with the temptation to sin, it's through Christ that we have received ultimate victory over sin's power.

Reflection:

What effect does Adam's original sin have on us, and what effect does the righteousness of Jesus have on us?

_____

_____

Why was the law given and what relationship does it have with sin?

_____

_____

Prayer Prompt:

Take a moment to thank God that we are not bound by the law. Thank him for his sacrifice and that through it we can enjoy the victory over sin's power.

WEEK 4 - DAY 5

Scripture Reading - Romans 6:1-7

[1] What shall we say, then? Shall we go on sinning so that grace may increase? [2] By no means! We are those who have died to sin; how can we live in it any longer? [3] Or don't you know that all of us who were baptized into Christ Jesus were baptized into his death? [4] We were therefore buried with him through baptism into death in order that, just as Christ was raised from the dead through the glory of the Father, we too may live a new life. [5] For if we have been united with him in a death like his, we will certainly also be united with him in a resurrection like his. [6] For we know that our old self was crucified with him so that the body ruled by sin might be done away with, that we should no longer be slaves to sin— [7] because anyone who has died has been set free from sin.

Commentary:

Romans 6 marks the beginning of a new section in Paul's letter that shifts the focus from justification (the moment that a sinner is declared righteous) to sanctification (the ongoing process of living more like Christ after the moment of salvation). This next section (chapters 6-8) will unpack what life looks like after being declared righteous through faith.

Paul begins this section by addressing a very important question that he anticipates his readers might be thinking: "If our eternity is secured by our faith in Jesus, then does that give me the freedom to do whatever I want, even if it's sinful? If grace abounds, then am I free to keep sinning?"

Paul answers this question emphatically by saying, "By no means! We are those who have died to sin; how can we live in it any longer?" Paul uses the powerful analogy of death to communicate that the one who has been justified by faith cannot continue to live as they please. Since we have been united with Christ in such a transformative way, it should be our desire to walk and follow him as we pursue holiness.

Our union with Christ is not simply experienced with him in his death, but also with him in his life as well. Christ died for our sins and now, through faith in Christ, the people we were before he saved us are no more! When Christ rose from the grave and when we believed, we also rose with him into a new life and are no longer controlled by sin.

This is the point Paul is making when he says, "For if we have been united with him in a death like his, we will certainly also be united with him in a resurrection like his." To die to something is to remove that thing, and its influence, from your life. Therefore, when, by faith, we die to our sin, we are freed from its influence over us. Now, as followers of Christ, our desire is to not live according to the flesh but according to the Spirit who is at work in us.

Reflection:

How does being united with Christ through His death change our relationship to sin?

_____

_____

If we are now dead to sin, why do we still struggle so much? What can you do to fight against the temptations of sin in your life?

_____

_____

Prayer Prompt:

Thank God for the new life you have through Christ. Also, spend some time confessing the things that may be sin in your life that need to be done away with.

WEEK 5 - DAY 1

Scripture Reading - Romans 6:8-14

[8] Now if we died with Christ, we believe that we will also live with him. [9] For we know that since Christ was raised from the dead, he cannot die again; death no longer has mastery over him. [10] The death he died, he died to sin once for all; but the life he lives, he lives to God.

[11] In the same way, count yourselves dead to sin but alive to God in Christ Jesus. [12] Therefore do not let sin reign in your mortal body so that you obey its evil desires. [13] Do not offer any part of yourself to sin as an instrument of wickedness, but rather offer yourselves to God as those who have been brought from death to life; and offer every part of yourself to him as an instrument of righteousness. [14] For sin shall no longer be your master, because you are not under the law, but under grace.

Commentary:

At the coronation of King Charles III, Prince William, son of the newly crowned monarch, knelt before his father and pledged the *Homage of Royal Blood* by saying, "I, William, Prince of Wales, pledge my loyalty to you, and faith and truth I will bear unto you, as your liege man of life and limb. So help me God." With these words, Prince William promised to serve the king with all fidelity of his life and person. A very similar oath was recited by Prince William's grandfather, Prince Phillip, at the coronation of his wife, Queen Elizabeth II, in June 1953. Solemn pledges of total allegiance, support, and loyalty are common at the coronations of sovereigns, both past and present.

In today's reading, the Apostle Paul exhorts Christians to walk in the liberation of the death of sin and the identification of the resurrected life found in Christ. Paul speaks of sin no longer being "master" (6:14) of believers, and he implores us not to let sin "reign" (6:12) in any part of our lives. Interestingly, Paul does not write that believers should not let sin "live" in our bodies. Rather, he says Christians should not let sin "reign" in our bodies. When sin takes up residence in our lives, it does not quarantine influence to only one space. Sin becomes like a tyrannical monarch, demanding pledges of total allegiance to its wicked rule. While unable to alter the eternity of the saved soul, on earth, sin still wants not to merely reside, but to rule and reign in the life of the believer. Paul implores us to live as though we are "dead to sin," (6:11) not giving in to its demand for control. Christ-followers must not allow the demonic monarchy of sin to cause us to be "instruments of wickedness," but rather, we must offer all of who we are to God as "instruments of righteousness." (6:13) The power to depose sin from the throne of influence in the believer's life is undertaken by walking in gratitude that the oppressive condemnation of the law has been replaced by the life-giving freedom of grace. Through grace, Christians are no longer condemned by the law — we are liberated by our reigning sovereign, King Jesus, who saves us.

Reflection:

What are some of the ways you have seen sin become like a selfish reigning monarch or tyrannical master in your life or the life of someone you know?

_____

_____

What does it mean to "offer every part of yourself to [God] as an instrument of righteousness?" How can you do this today?

_____

_____

Prayer Prompt:

Thank God that, through the overflowing grace of the death of Jesus, you serve a king who frees you rather than a master who binds you.

WEEK 5 - DAY 2

Scripture Reading - Romans 6:15-23

[15] What then? Shall we sin because we are not under the law but under grace? By no means! [16] Don't you know that when you offer yourselves to someone as obedient slaves, you are slaves of the one you obey—whether you are slaves to sin, which leads to death, or to obedience, which leads to righteousness? [17] But thanks be to God that, though you used to be slaves to sin, you have come to obey from your heart the pattern of teaching that has now claimed your allegiance. [18] You have been set free from sin and have become slaves to righteousness.

[19] I am using an example from everyday life because of your human limitations. Just as you used to offer yourselves as slaves to impurity and to ever-increasing wickedness, so now offer yourselves as slaves to righteousness leading to holiness. [20] When you were slaves to sin, you were free from the control of righteousness. [21] What benefit did you reap at that time from the things you are now ashamed of? Those things result in death! [22] But now that you have been set free from sin and have become slaves of God, the benefit you reap leads to holiness, and the result is eternal life. [23] For the wages of sin is death, but the gift of God is eternal life in Christ Jesus our Lord.

Commentary:

On June 19, 1865, Union soldiers marched into Galveston, Texas, the final stop of their historical journey. By the power of the Thirteenth Amendment, this day marked the last declaration of the abolition of slavery in the United States, granting freedom to over a quarter of a million slaves in Texas. Finally and fully, they were truly free at last. Jubilant celebrations and newborn freedom were met with immediate uncertainty by those whose chains had been loosed. What would men and women who spent their entire lives as slaves do? Owning no homes or property, where would they live? Where would they work? Could they vote? Hold political office? Start businesses? Emancipation was welcomed by these former slaves, but many questions remained about how their newfound freedom would be expressed and received. While slaves were legally lifted from slavery, much was unknown about how the effects of slavery would be lifted from slaves.

Much like liberated slaves, Christians struggle to live as though sin is dead and as though they are alive in Christ. In the words of Martyn

Lloyd Jones, "You can be a slave, experientially, even when you are no longer a slave legally."1 In the same way, Christians can live as slaves experientially, even when we are no longer slaves spiritually. How can a person be freed in principle and in practice from the slavery of sin? Paul makes clear that humans will become slaves to something. Either we become slaves to sin, which leads to shame, or we become slaves to righteousness, which leads to holiness and eternal life. (6:19-20) Christians must choose to walk in obedience, which makes us slaves of a loving master who will bring us freedom, not the impurity or wickedness brought upon us by the depraved master of sin. This gift of freedom is not something earned; it is received only through the atoning death of Christ Jesus. (6:23) Therefore, as a Christian, do not live as though you are a slave to sin. Live as a slave to righteousness by the rescue and salvation imparted by the death of Jesus.

Reflection:

A common desire for all humans is the desire for control. How does it make you feel when Paul says that, if you belong to Christ, you have become a slave of righteousness (Romans 6:19)?

What are some differences between being a slave to sin (Romans 6:17) and a slave to God (Romans 6:22)? How are God and sin different masters?

Prayer Prompt:

Ask God what righteousness looks like in an area of your life that might not currently be in line with what honors him. Next, ask God to give you the courage to become a slave to righteousness in that space.

WEEK 5 - DAY 3

Scripture Reading - Romans 7:1-6

¹ Do you not know, brothers and sisters—for I am speaking to those who know the law—that the law has authority over someone only as long as that person lives? ² For example, by law a married woman is bound to her husband as long as he is alive, but if her husband dies, she is released from the law that binds her to him. ³ So then, if she has sexual relations with another man while her husband is still alive, she is called an adulteress. But if her husband dies, she is released from that law and is not an adulteress if she marries another man.

⁴ So, my brothers and sisters, you also died to the law through the body of Christ, that you might belong to another, to him who was raised from the dead, in order that we might bear fruit for God. ⁵ For when we were in the realm of the flesh, the sinful passions aroused by the law were at work in us, so that we bore fruit for death. ⁶ But now, by dying to what once bound us, we have been released from the law so that we serve in the new way of the Spirit, and not in the old way of the written code.

Commentary:

Great communicators love great illustrations. Whether it is a story of heroic bravery resulting in victory, tragedy turning into triumph, or a hopelessly lost cause being miraculously redeemed, great illustrations help both the audience and the communicator understand complex ideas by comparison with real-life examples that are naturally and more easily understood.

In today's passage, Paul again answers his question, "Shall we sin because we are not under the law but under grace?" (Romans 6:15) by giving an example to illustrate the relationship between Christian liberty and the new life found in Christ. In Romans 6:16-22, Paul first illustrated the choice believers make between being a slave to sin or a slave to righteousness. Then, at the beginning of Romans 7, Paul offers a second illustration to the question in Romans 6:15 by comparing a wife to a widow. A wife is bound to certain obligations due to the vows she has taken. In the case of a widow, she is released from those obligations. Paul illustrates that believers will be "married" to either the law or to Christ. His implication is there is no "unmarried" spiritual state. One is either united to the law, which condemns us, or united to Christ, who frees us. Just as a wife is released from the covenant of marriage when her husband dies, so when we are united with Christ in salvation, a believer dies to the law (7:4) and is released from the condemnation of the law. Taking the illustration further, just as a husband and wife may bear children during their marriage, our unification with the law, before uniting with Christ, produces "fruit for death" (7:5). However, being united with Christ "bears fruit for God" (7:4) and serving "in the new way of the spirit" (7:6). A believer's unity in Christ is not to be viewed as an obligation or burden. On the contrary, like a happy and healthy marriage, the freedoms lost in our unification with Christ are far surpassed by the riches of knowing, being known, and living in the contentment of being the beloved of God.

Reflection:

Why does Paul use the image of "fruit" in this passage? If you are united to Christ, what are some examples of "fruit for God" (7:4) in your life?

_____

_____

What are some ways that belonging to Christ (7:4) frees us rather than binds us?

_____

_____

Prayer Prompt:

Find a still and quiet place. In solitude, ask God to reveal any area in your life where you are bearing "fruit for death" rather than "fruit for God." Rest your mind, still your heart and wait to hear him speak. Respond with repentance to whatever he reveals. Now, walk in the freedom that he gives through death to the law made possible by the death and resurrection of Christ.

WEEK 5 - DAY 4

Scripture Reading - Romans 7:7-12

[7] What shall we say, then? Is the law sinful? Certainly not! Nevertheless, I would not have known what sin was had it not been for the law. For I would not have known what coveting really was if the law had not said, "You shall not covet." [8] But sin, seizing the opportunity afforded by the commandment, produced in me every kind of coveting. For apart from the law, sin was dead. [9] Once I was alive apart from the law; but when the commandment came, sin sprang to life and I died. [10] I found that the very commandment that was intended to bring life actually brought death. [11] For sin, seizing the opportunity afforded by the commandment, deceived me, and through the commandment put me to death. [12] So then, the law is holy, and the commandment is holy, righteous and good.

Commentary:

Paul repeats his pattern of opening a section of Scripture by asking the reader a question, "Is the law sinful?" (7:7) With this rhetorical question, Paul anticipates that after reading previous sections discussing the nature of the law and its influence in the life of the believer (Romans 6:1-7:6) the reader might conclude that the law itself is evil. Paul quickly makes clear that the law is not evil by clarifying its purpose. The beginning purpose of the law is to define sin to us (7:7). However, not only does the law define sin to us, it also reveals the depth of the sin that lies within us (7:8).

Have you ever touched a searing hot pan? Instantly and unforgettably, blistering heat transferred from the heat source to the pan, to your skin, to your nerves, to your brain, and you snatched your hand away in pain. At that moment, the laws of thermodynamics defined heat for you, and it was revealed by the workings of those laws that heat had affected you. While you might not have known the specific scientific laws governing heat transference, you experientially came to understand the undeniable reality of heat as well as the consequences of touching a searing pan. The laws of convection, conduction, and radiation are not evil. Rather, they define and reveal the nature and result of heat. Such is the same with the law of God and its definition and revelation of sin.

Going further, Paul reveals something more sinister that happens once the law defines and reveals sin. He explains that once an understanding of coveting was revealed to him, the nature of sin at work within him "produced...every kind of coveting." (7:8) Thus, the law uncovers our deeper brokenness to desire to do wrong simply for the sake of doing wrong. In our fallen nature, "forbidden fruit" becomes momentarily delectable not merely for its satisfying taste but even more so, for sinful delight in its forbidden status. Thus, the law of God exposes, perhaps, the strongest appeal of sin in all mankind—our desire for control. We want sovereignty over our choices and determination of our consequences. We want to be God. Acceptance of this inborn desire leads to the revelation that evil does not reside within the law of God, but rather, evil resides within the heart of man.

Reflection:

How does understanding the purpose of the law change how you think about sin?

_____

_____

Reflect on a time in your life when it seemed as if you or someone you know did wrong for the sake of doing wrong. What can you learn from understanding this tendency in the human heart?

_____

_____

Prayer Prompt:

Thank God for his "holy, righteous, and good" (7:12) laws. Ask him to reveal where you have allowed your spirit to be put to death (7:11) by being deceived by sin. Thank him for the revelation of the places of brokenness, and ask him to help you move forward in the new life found in him.

WEEK 5 - DAY 5

Scripture Reading - Romans 7:13-25

[13] Did that which is good, then, become death to me? By no means! Nevertheless, in order that sin might be recognized as sin, it used what is good to bring about my death, so that through the commandment sin might become utterly sinful.

[14] We know that the law is spiritual; but I am unspiritual, sold as a slave to sin. [15] I do not understand what I do. For what I want to do I do not do, but what I hate I do. [16] And if I do what I do not want to do, I agree that the law is good. [17] As it is, it is no longer I myself who do it, but it is sin living in me. [18] For I know that good itself does not dwell in me, that is, in my sinful nature. For I have the desire to do what is good, but I cannot carry it out. [19] For I do not do the good I want to do, but the evil I do not want to do—this I keep on doing. [20] Now if I do what I do not want to do, it is no longer I who do it, but it is sin living in me that does it.

[21] So I find this law at work: Although I want to do good, evil is right there with me. [22] For in my inner being I delight in God's law; [23] but I see another law at work in me, waging war against the law of my mind and making me a prisoner of the law of sin at work within me. [24] What a wretched man I am! Who will rescue me from this body that is subject to death? [25] Thanks be to God, who delivers me through Jesus Christ our Lord! So then, I myself in my mind am a slave to God's law, but in my sinful nature a slave to the law of sin.

Commentary:

Have you ever needed to save more money? Ever knew you should go to the gym? Have you ever decided that it's time to eat healthier? Thought that you should go to bed earlier or spend less time on social media? Generally speaking, humans never accidentally do anything good. We never accidentally save money, go to the gym, eat healthier, get in bed early, or put down our phones. On the contrary, we might feel as if we accidentally spent too much money, gained weight, lost fitness, or wasted time. If you've ever "accidentally" found yourself in an activity or consequence where you asked, "How did I get here?" you might be encouraged to realize that you are in good company. The apostle Paul experienced the same frustration between his desire to do good and his sinful nature.

How can believers reconcile the contradictory forces at war within their hearts and minds? Paul writes that there are two laws at work within him and within each of us: the law of God (7:21-22), which Paul delights in and desires to honor, and the law of sin (7:23), which produces an evil pull toward unrighteousness. For the believer, even though the eternal status of the soul is settled by salvation, the attraction of sin still wars against our new identity found in Christ. However, Paul does not conclude the section in despair over his consistent inability to do that which he wishes to do. Rather, he concludes by acknowledging the wretchedness of his sinful state (7:24) and by praising God for his continual act of deliverance through Christ. While victory over the law of sin will only be final when believers step into eternity, here-and-now freedom is made possible by the redeeming, delivering death of Christ Jesus. (7:25) Thus, moment by moment, we may be empowered to live as a slave to the law of God rather than as a slave to the law of sin.

Reflection:

In what areas of your life do you find yourself doing what you wish you were not doing? Likewise, in what areas of your life do you find yourself not doing what you wish you were doing? What does Paul teach us about this contradiction of desires?

_____

_____

What first step do you need to take to find deliverance from the law of sin in your life today?

_____

_____

Prayer Prompt:

Acknowledge to God your inability to be consistent with your desires to please him. Ask him to fight the war in your mind and to break the power of the law of sin in your life. Thank God that you have victory and deliverance through Christ, both now and into eternity.

WEEK 6 - DAY 1

Scripture Reading - Romans 8:1-4

[1] Therefore, there is now no condemnation for those who are in Christ Jesus, [2] because through Christ Jesus the law of the Spirit who gives life has set you free from the law of sin and death. [3] For what the law was powerless to do because it was weakened by the flesh, God did by sending his own Son in the likeness of sinful flesh to be a sin offering. And so he condemned sin in the flesh, [4] in order that the righteous requirement of the law might be fully met in us, who do not live according to the flesh but according to the Spirit.

Commentary:

In the first 5 chapters of Romans, Paul addressed the question of how sinful people deserving condemnation could be declared righteous by a Holy God. In Romans 6 and 7, Paul discussed the ongoing struggle that Christians face as they continue to wrestle with sin and the pull of "the flesh" in their life, despite their status as those who have been justified (declared righteous). But now, in chapter 8, in light of that ongoing struggle, Paul reminds his readers of the glorious benefits of their justification that far outweigh their struggles as they continue to "work out" their salvation.

Right out of the gate, Paul reminds his readers that in spite of their ongoing struggles with sin, there is no condemnation for those who believe. Beyond that fact, the news gets better - through Jesus we have been set free from our sin. Not only are we not condemned for our sin, we are free from it. That means we are not chained to it anymore, that we are not owned by it anymore, and that we are not controlled by it anymore because of what has taken place in the life of those who have been declared righteous by God through faith. That's the key. Paul is explaining that Jesus has declared us legally free from the law of sin and death eternally. Jesus also unlocked the jail cell of sin, so we're no longer locked inside it. The question is whether we will trust him enough to walk out of the familiar jail cell of sin that used to be our home. On our own, this is impossible, but because of the sacrifice of Jesus and the power of the Holy Spirit living inside those who follow him, we have a new life of freedom from the condemnation we once deserved.

Reflection:

Today, what is one area of your life you can intentionally practice trusting and living in the Spirit and not your own flesh?

_____

_____

Prayer Prompt:

Pray for the Spirit to reveal areas that you're still living according to your flesh and not his Spirit, and then for boldness to trust him and walk in his way every hour of the day.

WEEK 6 - DAY 2

Scripture Reading - Romans 8:5-8

⁵ Those who live according to the flesh have their minds set on what the flesh desires; but those who live in accordance with the Spirit have their minds set on what the Spirit desires. ⁶ The mind governed by the flesh is death, but the mind governed by the Spirit is life and peace. ⁷ The mind governed by the flesh is hostile to God; it does not submit to God's law, nor can it do so. ⁸ Those who are in the realm of the flesh cannot please God.

Commentary:

If you've ever tried paddleboarding, you know it requires a lot of balance and focus to stay on top of the board instead of swimming beside it. The trick is to know where to focus. Our natural tendency is to look at the board where our feet are because that's the closest and seemingly best way to affect our balance. Unfortunately, that's the exact opposite of what will keep you balanced on the paddleboard. The best way to keep balance is actually to focus on the horizon. When we focus on the horizon, it calibrates our brains to something steady and unmoving, therefore enabling the rest of our body to keep balanced (and dry).

In a similar way, Paul is encouraging us to focus on what is true and steady and unmoving - the Spirit of God and what he desires instead of what we desire. The problem is, when we focus so much on ourselves and our circumstances, we lose sight of God's perspective. When we lose sight of his perspective, our body calibrates on whatever shiny thing comes across our path. Our sinful nature points us towards what is temporary and destructive, but the Lord's way is life-giving and eternal. Our sinful nature drags us into hostility with God, but his way leads to true peace and true unity with him. Colossians 3:1-2 echoes this passage when it reads, "Since, then, you have been raised with Christ, set your hearts on things above, where Christ is, seated at the right hand of God. Set your minds on things above, not on earthly things." Therefore, our hearts must abide in and our minds must focus on Christ and Christ alone.

Reflection:

What is one specific way you tend to focus on living "according to the flesh" in your life instead of "according to the Spirit?"

_____

_____

What are some practical steps to daily shift your focus from the temporary and destructive desires of the flesh to the life-giving and eternal desires of the Spirit?

_____

_____

Prayer Prompt:

Pray for the Spirit to renew your mind today and focus your desires towards him.

WEEK 6 - DAY 3

Scripture Reading - Romans 8:9-11

⁹ You, however, are not in the realm of the flesh but are in the realm of the Spirit, if indeed the Spirit of God lives in you. And if anyone does not have the Spirit of Christ, they do not belong to Christ. ¹⁰ But if Christ is in you, then even though your body is subject to death because of sin, the Spirit gives life because of righteousness. ¹¹ And if the Spirit of him who raised Jesus from the dead is living in you, he who raised Christ from the dead will also give life to your mortal bodies because of his Spirit who lives in you.

Commentary:

Who are we? What makes up our identity? Are we the name we're given? Are we the language we speak? Are we our nationality, or team, or our school? What makes us who we are? Humans, for better or worse, tend to group ourselves together based on similarities. We then take cues from that group about how to act and what values to adhere to. For example, we may tend to group together by political party, or a team we cheer for, or the school we attend. But are those things really the worthy answer to the question asked above, "Who are we?"

In contrast to our way of doing things, God doesn't group us by our affiliations, he only groups humans based on one criteria: who we belong to. So the question, "Who are we?" is actually not the fundamental question we should be asking. The question should be, "Whose are we?" Paul writes, "...if Christ is in you, then even though your body is subject to death because of sin, the Spirit gives life because of righteousness (8:10)." If righteousness can only be attained by belonging to Christ, then we should base who we are on whose we are, because that changes everything.

In addition to the reminder that we belong to Christ, this passage reveals to us that when we belong to Christ, we receive the unbelievable gift of the very presence of God, the Holy Spirit, living within us (verse 9). In Romans 6 and 7 Paul discussed the ongoing struggle that Christians face with sin and "the flesh" even after they have been declared righteous. But now, in chapter 8, Paul reminds his readers that we do not face this struggle alone - the very Spirit of God lives within all who have been declared righteous. And the Spirit gives each believer the power to live in accordance with our identity as ones who belong to Christ.

Reflection:

How does understanding our identity in terms of "whose we are" rather than "who we are" affect the way we view ourselves and our purpose in life?

_____

_____

In what ways have you experienced the Holy Spirit empowering you to live in accordance with your identity in Christ?

_____

_____

Prayer Prompt:

Thank the Lord for the gift of the Holy Spirit and pray that the Spirit would permeate every part of your day and reflect the truth that you belong to Christ.

WEEK 6 - DAY 4

Scripture Reading - Romans 8:12-17

[12] Therefore, brothers and sisters, we have an obligation—but it is not to the flesh, to live according to it. [13] For if you live according to the flesh, you will die; but if by the Spirit you put to death the misdeeds of the body, you will live. [14] For those who are led by the Spirit of God are the children of God. [15] The Spirit you received does not make you slaves, so that you live in fear again; rather, the Spirit you received brought about your adoption to sonship. And by him we cry, " Abba, Father." [16] The Spirit himself testifies with our spirit that we are God's children. [17] Now if we are children, then we are heirs—heirs of God and co-heirs with Christ, if indeed we share in his sufferings in order that we may also share in his glory.

Commentary:

To have been adopted by God implies that at some point, we did not belong to him. We weren't his son or his daughter. We were homeless children without direction or someone to care for us. We were as good as dead. But now, if we have given our will and our life to Jesus, then in return he has given us a home, guidance in all things, and a love that surpasses our understanding. Paul writes that we're given "sonship," which (whether male or female) gives us the legal, spiritual rights and inheritance of a child of God. That's a title that may lose its meaning if we don't stop and consider it, but if we ponder the weight of that gift, then we have no proper response aside from gratitude, worship, and obedience. We were slaves and now we are children. We were enemies and now we are children. We were outcasts and now, by God's grace, we are children.

There is an old church hymn lyric that goes like this, *"Trust and obey, for there's no other way, to be happy in Jesus, but to trust and obey."* It's a simple melody and rhyme that communicates an important truth: to trust God is to obey him. If we trust that we are his children, then we obey what he's laid out as best for us, and most importantly, his kingdom. Unfortunately because we still carry this sin nature within us, we often divorce trust from obedience. We trust that we are loved and are God's children, but we don't obey his wisdom or his calling. We trust we've been set free from our slavery to sin, but don't obey his advice to flee from it. Paul writes, "brothers and sisters, we have an obligation…," an obligation to live according to his Spirit that flows from a heart of gratitude. We have been adopted and now belong to him, therefore as his children we should, as the hymn says, "trust and obey."

Reflection:

Why is it important to remember that we were once not part of God's family but now have been given full rights and inheritance as his children? How can this perspective influence our view of those that don't yet belong to him?

_____

_____

How do trust and obedience work together in your relationship with God? Can you identify areas in your life where you trust God but struggle to obey him?

_____

_____

Prayer Prompt:

Pray for the Spirit to remind you of your identity in Jesus and to trust his guidance, just as a child trusts a perfect father, rather than relying on your own understanding.

WEEK 6 - DAY 5

Scripture Reading - Romans 8:18-25

[18] I consider that our present sufferings are not worth comparing with the glory that will be revealed in us. [19] For the creation waits in eager expectation for the children of God to be revealed. [20] For the creation was subjected to frustration, not by its own choice, but by the will of the one who subjected it, in hope [21] that the creation itself will be liberated from its bondage to decay and brought into the freedom and glory of the children of God. [22] We know that the whole creation has been groaning as in the pains of childbirth right up to the present time. [23] Not only so, but we ourselves, who have the firstfruits of the Spirit, groan inwardly as we wait eagerly for our adoption to sonship, the redemption of our bodies. [24] For in this hope we were saved. But hope that is seen is no hope at all. Who hopes for what they already have? [25] But if we hope for what we do not yet have, we wait for it patiently.

Commentary:

Human beings are inherently short-sighted. In the grand scheme of things, our lives are but a blip, a vapor, and yet it seems nearly impossible to concentrate on anything before or after what's going on right in front of our eyes. That's why goals are so popular. They give a fixed target to focus on while enduring hard work or pain. Goals act as our proverbial carrot on the stick, and we need them because it's so unnatural for us to look beyond our circumstances.

In a much more significant way, this is what Paul is saying. He's helping this church in Rome (and us) to remember the goal and the promise laid out before us as believers and how our focus should be on the goal, not necessarily our circumstances. This goal is the promise of restoration for us and all of Creation that is to come. It's the promise of things that earth and humanity have groaned for since the very first act of sin. He writes, "our present sufferings are not worth comparing with the glory that will be revealed in us," (v. 18) and that, "the creation itself will be liberated from its bondage to decay and brought into the freedom and glory of the children of God" (v. 21). So with that in mind, the circumstances that seem to be yelling in our faces are, in fact, just a small hindrance to endure if we keep our eyes on the hope of what awaits us. Whether we're enduring hardship or we are in a season of comfort, these things aren't even worth mentioning in comparison with what God has ahead for those that have made him Lord and Savior. What an incredible hope we can rely on because of the sacrifice of Jesus!

Reflection:

How can you remind yourself daily of the future liberation and glory that Paul speaks about in Romans 8:18-25? What practical steps can you take to keep this hope at the forefront of your mind?

_____

_____

How does the hope of what's to come change the way you live and interact with others today? In what ways can you share this hope with those around you who might be struggling to see beyond their current circumstances?

_____

_____

Prayer Prompt:

Often gratitude is the antidote for discontentment, so today focus your prayer on thanking Jesus for the hope and the promise of restoration for all things, and the restoration of our lives.

WEEK 7 - DAY 1

Scripture Reading - Romans 8:26-27

[26] In the same way, the Spirit helps us in our weakness. We do not know what we ought to pray for, but the Spirit himself intercedes for us through wordless groans. [27] And he who searches our hearts knows the mind of the Spirit, because the Spirit intercedes for God's people in accordance with the will of God.

Commentary:

Up to this point in Romans chapter 8, Paul reminds the reader that those who have been declared righteous by God do not need to fear condemnation from God, as they have been filled with the very presence of God himself, the Holy Spirit. Paul also reminds the reader that those who are filled with the Spirit are to live in line with the Spirit, and not the flesh. But Paul has also acknowledged the struggle that humans have living in the "in between," as they look back at the work that Christ has already accomplished, but still long for the ultimate glory of God to be revealed at the end of this age. In fact, the brokenness of creation that resulted from the sin of man leads to creation "groaning as in the pains of childbirth" (8:22). Humans "groan" as well, perpetually reminded of the curse both present in their bodies and so evident in the world around them.

But after covering all of this, Paul lets the readers know that they are not the only ones who are groaning. Apparently, the Holy Spirit is groaning as well. However, unlike the groanings of creation and humanity which are primarily an outcry from suffering and pain, the groaning of the Holy Spirit is one of intercession, the act of praying on behalf of another person. Paul writes, "the Spirit himself intercedes for us through wordless groans." The Holy Spirit, the third member of the Triune God, is in constant communication with the Father, the first member of the Triune God. The Holy Spirit is actively and continually praying on the behalf of God's people.

At times the pains of this world may feel so overwhelming and difficult to bear that we, in our weakness, do not even know how or what to pray to God. And yet, in those moments, the very Spirit of God intercedes on the behalf of the believer - lifting up the believer with wordless groans that are always heard by the Father and are always in perfect alignment with the will of God. These perfect prayers are another glorious benefit for those who have been justified by God and are now indwelled by his life-giving Spirit.

Reflection:

Has there ever been a moment or season in life where you felt so overwhelmed that you weren't even sure how to pray? What was that season like?

_____

_____

What is your reaction to the revelation in this passage that the Holy Spirit intercedes on your behalf when you don't know how to pray yourself?

_____

_____

Prayer Prompt:

Thank the Holy Spirit for praying on your behalf when you don't know what to pray.

WEEK 7 - DAY 2

Scripture Reading - Romans 8:28-30
[28] And we know that in all things God works for the good of those who love him, who have been called according to his purpose. [29] For those God foreknew he also predestined to be conformed to the image of his Son, that he might be the firstborn among many brothers and sisters. [30] And those he predestined, he also called; those he called, he also justified; those he justified, he also glorified.

Commentary:

Even after acknowledging the brokenness of this present world and the brokenness of our present state as humans due to sin, Paul pens one of the most famous verses in all of Scripture. "In all things God works for the good of those who love him, who have been called according to his purpose" (8:28). In the midst of all creation and humanity groaning, longing for their day of ultimate restoration, Paul reminds his readers that God is still working out everything for good.

The verses in today's reading remind us of God's ultimate sovereignty and goodness in the midst of any and every situation we face. This concept that God is working out all things ultimately for good is found throughout the Scriptures. For example, when Joseph's brothers sold him into slavery it was an evil act committed by broken and jealous people. Yet, God used this very event to place Joseph in Egypt where he could interpret Pharaoh's dream and prepare the nation of Egypt to store food that would sustain Joseph's family through a terrible famine. This allowed Joseph to say to his brothers at the end of his life, "You intended to harm me, but God intended it for good to accomplish what is now being done, the saving of many lives" (Genesis 50:20). Time and time again, God has proven that he is able to work all things out for the ultimate good of those who love him.

Today's reading is a promise to all who believe that no matter what situation you are going through, no matter how painful your current situation is, no matter how loudly you are groaning along with creation today, you can know that God will be faithful to complete everything that Paul has promised he would do in the first 8 chapters of this letter. All those who have put their faith in Jesus will continue to be conformed to the image of Jesus, and will one day be glorified with Him in accordance with God's unshakeable promises.

Reflection:

Can you think of a time when you went through a situation that felt difficult and painful at the time, but looking back, you can see that God used that situation for your ultimate good?

_____

_____

In light of these verses, how can you respond in those moments when your life is difficult and painful?

_____

_____

Prayer Prompt:

Give thanks to the Lord that he is in control of all things and that he is perpetually and continually working all events and all human decisions towards the ultimate good of those who love him.

WEEK 7 - DAY 3

Scripture Reading - Romans 8:31-39

[31] What, then, shall we say in response to these things? If God is for us, who can be against us? [32] He who did not spare his own Son, but gave him up for us all—how will he not also, along with him, graciously give us all things? [33] Who will bring any charge against those whom God has chosen? It is God who justifies. [34] Who then is the one who condemns? No one. Christ Jesus who died—more than that, who was raised to life—is at the right hand of God and is also interceding for us. [35] Who shall separate us from the love of Christ? Shall trouble or hardship or persecution or famine or nakedness or danger or sword? [36] As it is written:

> "For your sake we face death all day long;
> we are considered as sheep to be slaughtered."

[37] No, in all these things we are more than conquerors through him who loved us. [38] For I am convinced that neither death nor life, neither angels nor demons, neither the present nor the future, nor any powers, [39] neither height nor depth, nor anything else in all creation, will be able to separate us from the love of God that is in Christ Jesus our Lord.

Commentary:

After assuring his readers of God's promise to work out all things for the good of those who love Him, Paul addresses the unspoken question that he assumes is lingering in the minds of some of his readers. Some reading Paul's letter might say, "Paul, that sounds great and all, and I'm glad to hear that God is working out all things for good, but you have no idea what I'm going through. How could this be something that the Lord can use for good?" Someone in Paul's audience might be looking at their own situation and feel that it is hopeless - that there is no way that God could take a situation so difficult, so painful, or so evil, and somehow turn it out for good.

So Paul writes one of the most beautiful paragraphs in the entire book of Romans to assure every reader that no matter what situation, no matter what "trouble or hardship or persecution or famine or nakedness or danger or sword" we face in this world, God will never forsake us in the midst of it, because, "If God is for us, who can be against us?" Paul says no matter what situation you are facing, no matter what enemy you are facing, whether you are facing death or life, angels or demons, things in the present or things to come, any powers, height or depth, or anything else in all creation - nothing can separate you "from the love of God that is in Christ Jesus."

For those who have put their faith in God as revealed in Jesus Christ, they are "more than conquerors through Him." They are conquerors not because of their own strength, but because of the faithfulness and love of the one who delivered them from their bondage to sin and death. And whether the believer sees deliverance from their current situation in this life or in the next, the end result is guaranteed - those that God has justified will overcome.

Reflection:

What is your response to God's promise in this chapter that nothing could ever separate us from him?

_____

_____

How does remembering that promise impact your thought words and actions today?

_____

_____

Prayer Prompt:

Ask the Lord to remind you in moments of worry or suffering that His promises are true and nothing can ever separate us from His love for us.

WEEK 7 - DAY 4

Scripture Reading - Romans 9:1-5

¹ I speak the truth in Christ—I am not lying, my conscience confirms it through the Holy Spirit— ² I have great sorrow and unceasing anguish in my heart. ³ For I could wish that I myself were cursed and cut off from Christ for the sake of my people, those of my own race, ⁴ the people of Israel. Theirs is the adoption to sonship; theirs the divine glory, the covenants, the receiving of the law, the temple worship and the promises. ⁵ Theirs are the patriarchs, and from them is traced the human ancestry of the Messiah, who is God over all, forever praised! Amen.

Commentary:

Welcome to Romans chapters 9-11, three of the most debated and potentially difficult chapters in all of Scripture to understand. We encourage you to view these three chapters as one cohesive unit that will help provide a more complete picture of what Paul is saying when taken as a whole. In the very first chapter of Paul's letter, in the "theme verse" of the book, Paul writes, "For I am not ashamed of the gospel, because it is the power of God that brings salvation to everyone who believes: first to the Jew, then to the Gentile" (Romans 1:16). In Romans 9-11, Paul is going to focus his attention on the last portion of that verse - "first for the Jew, then to the Gentile." Writing to a group of Christians in Rome that consists of both Jews and Gentiles, Paul addresses how God's plan has always included both groups and how these two groups have been brought into the one family of God.

To begin this section, Paul shares with the reader his heartbreak over the response of his Jewish brothers and sisters to the gospel as revealed in Jesus Christ. As Paul has been traveling the world for a number of years at this point sharing the gospel, he has observed a pattern that deeply saddens him. In most cities, it is the Gentiles who are responding positively to the gospel message. The Jews in these cities are primarily rejecting Jesus as their Messiah and refusing to believe that God would allow Gentiles into the family of God. In this section, Paul says that if there were anyone who should have recognized Jesus as the Messiah-as God in the flesh-it was the Jews. They had all of the advantages of the covenants, the law, and the temple - things that were meant to point them to the eventual arrival of Jesus as their Messiah. And yet, while some Jews had accepted Christ as their Messiah, the majority had not.

Paul is heartbroken over this. He is so heartbroken that he says in verse 3, if it were possible to give up his place in the family of God so that his Jewish brothers and sisters could take his place, he would do it! What is most remarkable is that the Jews have caused Paul the most trouble and persecution over the past years of his ministry, and yet, Paul's love for his people has never wavered. He puts into practice what Jesus commanded when he said that his followers are to love their enemies and pray for those who persecute them (Matthew 5:44).

Reflection:

Paul is heartbroken over the people in his life who do not know Jesus, even those who have caused him great pain. What is your attitude towards those in your life who don't know Jesus and have even caused you pain in your past?

_____

_____

_____

Prayer Prompt:

Ask the Lord to give you a heart for those who don't know Jesus, especially those who have wronged or persecuted you in the past.

WEEK 7 - DAY 5

Scripture Reading - Romans 9:6-13

[6] It is not as though God's word had failed. For not all who are descended from Israel are Israel. [7] Nor because they are his descendants are they all Abraham's children. On the contrary, "It is through Isaac that your offspring will be reckoned." [8] In other words, it is not the children by physical descent who are God's children, but it is the children of the promise who are regarded as Abraham's offspring. [9] For this was how the promise was stated: "At the appointed time I will return, and Sarah will have a son."

[10] Not only that, but Rebekah's children were conceived at the same time by our father Isaac. [11] Yet, before the twins were born or had done anything good or bad—in order that God's purpose in election might stand: [12] not by works but by him who calls—she was told, "The older will serve the younger." [13] Just as it is written: "Jacob I loved, but Esau I hated."

Commentary:

Up to this point in the book of Romans, Paul has made the case that God is the "just justifier." God was righteous in how he dealt with the sins of his people. He also allowed repentant sinners to be declared righteous and to receive the gift of eternal life using Christ's own righteousness. In these three chapters, Romans 9-11, Paul now turns to answer the question, "Was God righteous in how he dealt with the people of Israel? Did God keep His promises to the Jewish people?"

In verse 6 we see Paul's answer, "It is not as though God's word has failed." In the passages that follow, Paul demonstrates that it has always been God's plan to base his covenantal family on those who trust in him by faith alone-not on simply those who are related by blood lines or birthright. That means God's plan was always meant to include both Jews and Gentiles. For those Jewish people living in the first century this was a surprising truth. However, Paul makes the case that their very Scriptures foretold this truth.

To make this case, Paul goes back to the book of Genesis to demonstrate that not all descendants of Abraham, Isaac, and Jacob became a part of the covenantal family of God. Paul says, "not all who are descended from Israel are Israel," meaning that while many were physically descended from the Patriarchs, not all of those descendants were a part of the covenantal family of God. The clearest example of this in Paul's eyes is the birth and life of Jacob and Esau, twins born to Isaac and Rebekah. Both were clearly of the same blood line physically, and yet God, in his sovereign choice only had one of them be a part of the covenantal family. Paul then quotes Malachi 1:2-3 where the Lord says, "Jacob I loved, but Esau I hated." The use of "love" and "hate" in this passage are different from how we might use those words today. In their cultural context, these two words are covenant language terms. "Love" refers to God's covenantal faithfulness, but the word "hate" here refers to NOT being in a covenant relationship with. God showed great kindness to Esau throughout his life, but he was not the twin who was a part of the covenant.

Reflection:

Based on what we have read so far in the book of Romans, what would your response be to someone who said that they were a Christian because "they were born into a Christian family"?

_____

_____

Prayer Prompt:

Ask the Lord to give you wisdom and insight as you continue to read through Romans 9-11 and rejoice that God's plan has always included both Jews and Gentiles.

WEEK 8 - DAY 1

Scripture Reading - Romans 9:14-18

[14] What then shall we say? Is God unjust? Not at all! [15] For he says to Moses, "I will have mercy on whom I have mercy, and I will have compassion on whom I have compassion." [16] It does not, therefore, depend on human desire or effort, but on God's mercy. [17] For Scripture says to Pharaoh: "I raised you up for this very purpose, that I might display my power in you and that my name might be proclaimed in all the earth." [18] Therefore God has mercy on whom he wants to have mercy, and he hardens whom he wants to harden.

Commentary:

In the preceding verses, Paul argued that God's mercy was not given to all of Israel just because they were physical descendants of Abraham. Instead, God gave his mercy to those who were spiritual descendants of Abraham, Issac, and Jacob in faith, based on "God's purpose in election" (Romans 9:6-12). Paul then asks the question he knew his readers would likely be thinking: "If God chooses to only give his mercy to some and not to everyone, isn't he unjust?" Paul's answer is emphatic, "Not at all!" Paul knew what we often forget. We do not deserve God's mercy.

We go to church, we serve, we give to charity, we read our Bibles, and we pray. Then over time, we begin to subtly think "I am a pretty good person" and "I have done a lot of good." All of a sudden, whether we think it explicitly or not, we believe God owes us mercy. However, if God owes us mercy, then it cannot be mercy. Mercy is inherently undeserved, or else it would simply be a wage and Paul has already established that "all have sinned" (Romans 3:23) and "the wages of sin is death" (Romans 6:23). Therefore, each of us deserves death. We all are headed toward a broken and tragic ending…unless the mercy of God intervenes. Tim Keller wrote, "The shock is not that God does not extend his compassion to everyone, but that he extends it to anyone."[1]

It is good news then when Paul writes,"It does not depend on human desire or effort, but on God's mercy." In this verse, Paul humbles and draws the reader into worship at the same time. We cannot earn God's mercy and he does not owe us his mercy. Yet, the beauty is that God, in his sovereign goodness, has chosen to pour out his mercy on his people even though we don't deserve it.

Reflection:

What emotion do you feel when you reflect on the truth that God does not have to give mercy but chooses to give it to his people?

_____

_____

How can you share the mercy of God with someone else today?

_____

_____

Prayer Prompt:

Consider what it means to receive God's undeserved mercy. Take a moment to thank God for his undeserved mercy.

WEEK 8 - DAY 2

Scripture Reading - Romans 9:19-29

[19] One of you will say to me: "Then why does God still blame us? For who is able to resist his will?" [20] But who are you, a human being, to talk back to God? "Shall what is formed say to the one who formed it, 'Why did you make me like this?'" [21] Does not the potter have the right to make out of the same lump of clay some pottery for special purposes and some for common use?

[22] What if God, although choosing to show his wrath and make his power known, bore with great patience the objects of his wrath— prepared for destruction? [23] What if he did this to make the riches of his glory known to the objects of his mercy, whom he prepared in advance for glory— [24] even us, whom he also called, not only from the Jews but also from the Gentiles? [25] As he says in Hosea: "I will call them 'my people' who are not my people; and I will call her 'my loved one' who is not my loved one," [26] and, "In the very place where it was said to them, 'You are not my people,' there they will be called 'children of the living God.'"

[27] Isaiah cries out concerning Israel: "Though the number of the Israelites be like the sand by the sea, only the remnant will be saved. [28] For the Lord will carry out his sentence on earth with speed and finality." [29] It is just as Isaiah said previously: "Unless the Lord Almighty had left us descendants, we would have become like Sodom, we would have been like Gomorrah."

Commentary:

In this passage, Paul anticipates an age-old question that is also asked by many today. "How can God be in control of all things and we as humans still be responsible for our actions?" Paul's answer is not what we would expect. Instead of answering the question directly, Paul essentially says, "God is God and he can do as he pleases." To further make his point, he uses an Old Testament metaphor- God is the potter and we are the clay (Isaiah 29:15-16, 45:9, 64:8, and Jeremiah 18:1-12). Just as a potter can make anything he wants out of a lump of clay, so too can God make anything he wants out of us, his creation.

After this reminder of who God is and who we are, Paul gives us a clue into the mystery of God's mercy. He says that there are two types of people, "objects of wrath – prepared for destruction" and "objects of his mercy, whom he prepared in advance for glory." The objects of wrath are those who "suppress the truth" (Romans 1:18) and "neither glorify him as God nor give him thanks" (Romans 1:21). They refuse to believe and the result is that "God gave them over in the sinful desires of their hearts" (Romans 1:24). However, notice that Paul states very clearly that the "objects of mercy" are prepared by God. God works in the hearts of his people to soften their hearts so that they will come to believe in him. And all of this is "to make the riches of his glory known." God reveals himself to us so that we would see his glory and know his goodness. Then it is God who, in his loving control of all things, initiates and calls us to believe, and we respond by faith in Jesus to his mercy.

Reflection:

How have you felt God initiate and call you to a relationship with him?

_____

_____

What is our proper response to the reality that God is the one who initiates a relationship with us?

_____

_____

Prayer Prompt:

Meditate on and pray the words of Psalm 25: "Guide me in your truth and teach me, for you are God my Savior, and my hope is in you all day long. Remember, LORD, your great mercy and love, for they are from of old."

WEEK 8 - DAY 3

Scripture Reading - Romans 9:30-10:4

[30] What then shall we say? That the Gentiles, who did not pursue righteousness, have obtained it, a righteousness that is by faith; [31] but the people of Israel, who pursued the law as the way of righteousness, have not attained their goal. [32] Why not? Because they pursued it not by faith but as if it were by works. They stumbled over the stumbling stone. [33] As it is written:

> "See, I lay in Zion a stone that causes people to stumble
> and a rock that makes them fall,
> and the one who believes in him will never be put to shame."

[1] Brothers and sisters, my heart's desire and prayer to God for the Israelites is that they may be saved. [2] For I can testify about them that they are zealous for God, but their zeal is not based on knowledge. [3] Since they did not know the righteousness of God and sought to establish their own, they did not submit to God's righteousness. [4] Christ is the culmination of the law so that there may be righteousness for everyone who believes.

Commentary:

In the Old Testament, the Gentiles were the outsiders, the ones who did not believe in Yahweh, the God of Israel. Israel was God's chosen people, they were meant to be the stewards of God's Word. While there were examples of Gentiles coming to faith in God before Christ, such as Rahab and Ruth, there was a stark separation overall between the Gentiles and Jews. However, when Paul was writing this letter, the church in Rome had become increasingly made up of Gentiles. This was a shocking reversal. How is it that "the Gentiles, who did not pursue righteousness", responded to the gospel more than the Jews?

Paul says that it is because the Jews "pursued [righteousness] not by faith but as if it were by works." They believed they could be saved by adhering to the law. However, the law was given not as a means to earn salvation, but "to show people their sins" (Galatians 3:19 NLT). The Jews had put their hope in the law rather than putting their hope in Christ who "is the culmination of the law." This is why Paul says the Jews "stumbled over the stumbling stone." Jesus preached that salvation came only through "repenting and believing in the gospel" (Mark 1:15), but they "sought to establish their own [righteousness]," and, therefore, would not believe. The Gentiles, however, knew that their works would never be enough and they placed their faith in Jesus. This is the offense of the gospel. If we pursue salvation by works, even if we "are zealous for God," we will never attain it. However, if we abandon our attempts to earn salvation then we can find it in the finished work of Jesus. We trade in our self-righteousness to receive the all sufficient righteousness of Christ.

Reflection:

The Jews put their hope in the works of the law. What things in your life are you tempted to place your hope in?

_____

_____

What does it look like today to pursue righteousness by faith rather than by works?

_____

_____

Prayer Prompt:

Thank God for sending his son, Jesus, who "is the culmination of the law so that there may be righteousness for everyone who believes."

WEEK 8 - DAY 4

Scripture Reading - Romans 10:5-13

⁵ Moses writes this about the righteousness that is by the law: "The person who does these things will live by them." ⁶ But the righteousness that is by faith says: "Do not say in your heart, 'Who will ascend into heaven?'" (that is, to bring Christ down) ⁷ "or 'Who will descend into the deep?'" (that is, to bring Christ up from the dead). ⁸ But what does it say? "The word is near you; it is in your mouth and in your heart," that is, the message concerning faith that we proclaim: ⁹ If you declare with your mouth, "Jesus is Lord," and believe in your heart that God raised him from the dead, you will be saved. ¹⁰ For it is with your heart that you believe and are justified, and it is with your mouth that you profess your faith and are saved. ¹¹ As Scripture says, "Anyone who believes in him will never be put to shame." ¹² For there is no difference between Jew and Gentile—the same Lord is Lord of all and richly blesses all who call on him, ¹³ for, "Everyone who calls on the name of the Lord will be saved."

Commentary:

When we believe that we have to work for our salvation, there can never be rest or confidence in our faith. There will always be something that you could be doing that would make you better or more sure of your standing before God. We become slaves to our works as much as the Jews became slaves to the law. The good news of the gospel is that, through Jesus, we get to rest in his works. He is the one who has already descended from heaven, given himself for us on the cross, and then ascended from the grave and returned to heaven. The work is finished. So what do we do now that Jesus has already done the work?

"If you declare with your mouth, 'Jesus is Lord,' and believe in your heart that God raised him from the dead, you will be saved." We are called to respond in faith to the work of Jesus. It is important to remember that these statements are not merely words to be said or facts to be accepted, but they represent a new way of life. To say that "Jesus is Lord" is to surrender everything to him. All your hopes and dreams, all your money and possessions, it is all his. To "believe in your heart that God raised him from the dead" is to wholeheartedly place your trust in the life, death, and resurrection of Jesus. We are changed from the inside out-once sinners and now made dearly loved children of God.

Reflection:

What does it mean to let Jesus be Lord of your life?

_____

_____

What emotion do you feel when you reflect on the truth that Jesus has finished the work and now you can rest as a child of God?

_____

_____

Prayer Prompt:

Take a moment to ask Jesus to reveal to you any areas of your life where you have not allowed him to be Lord. Write these down and pray through each one asking God to help you surrender them to him. If you have never confessed Jesus as Lord of your life, this is the most important decision you will ever make and we invite you to make that confession today.

WEEK 8 - DAY 5

Scripture Reading - Romans 10:14-21

[14] How, then, can they call on the one they have not believed in? And how can they believe in the one of whom they have not heard? And how can they hear without someone preaching to them? [15] And how can anyone preach unless they are sent? As it is written: "How beautiful are the feet of those who bring good news!"

[16] But not all the Israelites accepted the good news. For Isaiah says, "Lord, who has believed our message?" [17] Consequently, faith comes from hearing the message, and the message is heard through the word about Christ. [18] But I ask: Did they not hear? Of course they did:

> "Their voice has gone out into all the earth,
>   their words to the ends of the world."

[19] Again I ask: Did Israel not understand? First, Moses says,
> "I will make you envious by those who are not a nation;
>   I will make you angry by a nation that has no understanding."

[20] And Isaiah boldly says,
> "I was found by those who did not seek me;
>   I revealed myself to those who did not ask for me."

[21] But concerning Israel he says,
> "All day long I have held out my hands
>   to a disobedient and obstinate people."

Commentary:

The gospel is for all people. Paul wrote, "Everyone who calls on the name of the Lord will be saved." However, Paul sees a problem. Anyone can call on Jesus and be saved, but they can't call on him unless they believe, and they can't believe unless they have heard about him. It doesn't end there, because people cannot hear about Jesus unless someone preaches to them. The gospel is for all people, and you are called to tell them the good news. There are currently more than three billion people in the world who have not been reached with the gospel. This means that they will be born, live, and die without knowing Jesus and his abundant love. On top of that, there are even more people who have heard the gospel and have not yet accepted the invitation. These people will end up in Hell...unless we do something about it. The mission can seem daunting but there are things that we can do today to help drive the mission forward.

Here are three things that we can do. First, we can pray for the Lord to use us to accomplish his mission to spread the gospel to all people. We cannot accomplish this mission without his power and presence. Second, we can give to organizations around the world who have committed to the work of reaching the lost. Third, we can go and share the gospel in our lives. "Going" does not necessarily mean leaving your state or country, though we should pray and ask God if he desires us to do so. "Going" starts by getting to know your neighbors and those who are in your life every day. Then you can show them the love of Jesus and open the door to preach the gospel to them. Remember Jesus's promise, "All authority in heaven and on earth has been given to me. Therefore go and make disciples of all nations, baptizing them in the name of the Father and of the Son and of the Holy Spirit, and teaching them to obey everything I have commanded you. And surely I am with you always, to the very end of the age" (Matthew 28:16-20).

Reflection:

How does it make you feel that Jesus has invited you to be a part of his mission to save the world?

_____

_____

Who is one person that you can pray for and seek to share the gospel with this week?

_____

_____

Prayer Prompt:

Take time to pray for those in the world who have not heard the gospel. Ask God to send people to preach the gospel so that they may hear, believe, and call on the name of Jesus.

WEEK 9 - DAY 1

Scripture Reading - Romans 11:1-10

¹ I ask then: Did God reject his people? By no means! I am an Israelite myself, a descendant of Abraham, from the tribe of Benjamin. ² God did not reject his people, whom he foreknew. Don't you know what Scripture says in the passage about Elijah—how he appealed to God against Israel: ³ "Lord, they have killed your prophets and torn down your altars; I am the only one left, and they are trying to kill me"? ⁴ And what was God's answer to him? "I have reserved for myself seven thousand who have not bowed the knee to Baal." ⁵ So too, at the present time there is a remnant chosen by grace. ²⁶ And if by grace, then it cannot be based on works; if it were, grace would no longer be grace.

⁷ What then? What the people of Israel sought so earnestly they did not obtain. The elect among them did, but the others were hardened, ⁸ as it is written:

> "God gave them a spirit of stupor,
>   eyes that could not see
>   and ears that could not hear,
> to this very day."
> ⁹ And David says:
> "May their table become a snare and a trap,
>   a stumbling block and a retribution for them.
> ¹⁰ May their eyes be darkened so they cannot see,
>   and their backs be bent forever."

Commentary:

Sometimes when we get caught up in our immediate circumstances, we fail to see the bigger picture. In light of the rejection of Jesus by many Jews, Paul asks, "Did God reject his people?" Paul anticipates that this question would come from Jewish believers in the church in Rome who felt alone as the church grew to include more and more Gentiles. To address this concern, Paul reminds his readers of a time in Israel's history when the prophet Elijah felt the same way.

In 1 Kings 18, Elijah boldly challenged the wicked king Ahab and his false prophets to a showdown. Elijah built an altar to Yahweh and hundreds of false prophets built an altar to their gods. Whoever's god responded with fire and consumed the altar was the superior god.

The false prophets cried out for hours, but nothing happened. They pleaded with their false gods from morning until evening with not even a spark on their altar. Unsurprised by their failure, Elijah went one step further. He had servants drench his altar with water three times. Then Elijah simply prayed for God to make himself known as the true God. Suddenly, fire fell from the sky and consumed the altar, including all the water that had been poured on it. Yahweh, the true God, victoriously made himself known.

Elijah should have basked in the moment, but he was forced to flee as King Ahab sought to kill him. From great victory to running for his life, Elijah felt the most alone he had ever felt and he let God know his feelings (1 Kings 19:10; Romans 11:3). But God told him, "You may not see it now but you are not alone, because I have kept a remnant of those faithful to me." Elijah was focused on his immediate circumstances, but God showed him the bigger picture. He was never truly alone because God never fails to faithfully keep his people.

That is Paul's message to the church in Rome and to all believers today. Even when it feels like everyone else has abandoned the faith and given up hope, remember there will always be a "remnant chosen by grace" who the Lord "will himself restore, confirm, strengthen, and establish" (1 Peter 5:10 ESV).

Reflection:

How does it give you hope that God himself keeps his people even in the darkest of times?

Prayer Prompt:

Pray for the Lord to remind you that he can see the entirety of his plan. Ask him to encourage you to be a part of his mission in the world instead of getting caught up in your immediate situation. Pray also for God to pour his abundant grace on believers around the world, especially in places where they are being persecuted for their faith.

WEEK 9 - DAY 2

Scripture Reading - Romans 11:11-16

[11] Again I ask: Did they stumble so as to fall beyond recovery? Not at all! Rather, because of their transgression, salvation has come to the Gentiles to make Israel envious. [12] But if their transgression means riches for the world, and their loss means riches for the Gentiles, how much greater riches will their full inclusion bring!

[13] I am talking to you Gentiles. Inasmuch as I am the apostle to the Gentiles, I take pride in my ministry [14] in the hope that I may somehow arouse my own people to envy and save some of them. [15] For if their rejection brought reconciliation to the world, what will their acceptance be but life from the dead? [16] If the part of the dough offered as firstfruits is holy, then the whole batch is holy; if the root is holy, so are the branches.

Commentary:

In this section, Paul continues to how the Jewish people in his day relate to God's plan of redemption. In the first 10 verses of this chapter, Paul makes the point that there has always been and will always be a remnant of Jewish people who continue to be faithful to God. Paul himself is an example of one of those people. In these verses, Paul addresses the rest of the Jews, who at this present moment are not a part of that remnant. As the Gentiles continue to pour into the family of God, is there any room for the Jewish people as well? Have the Jewish people as a whole rejected the Messiah to the point where they can never repent and return to the family of God? Paul's answer is clear and direct, "Not at all!" Paul believes that this stage of God's redemptive plan (an increase of Gentiles entering the kingdom) has been used by God to stir up an envy among the Jewish people so they can be confronted with their rejection of the Messiah and repent and return.

This passage reminds us of one of Jesus' most famous parables found in Luke 15:11-32, the story of the Prodigal Son. In this parable Jesus speaks of a father who had two sons. The younger son rejected his family, demanded his inheritance from his very alive and living father, and left home to squander his money with wild living. However, after he had spent everything and a great famine swept over the land, the younger son returned in shame to try to beg for forgiveness. And yet, the father received his son back to him and welcomed him immediately into the family and celebrated his return. On the other hand, the older son was not pleased at the father for welcoming back his sinful brother so quickly. The older brother was appalled by the father's forgiveness, and the older son demanded that he should be recognized and appreciated by the father for his faithfulness. The parable ends with the Father saying to the older son, "You are always with me, and everything I have is yours. But we had to celebrate and be glad, because this brother of yours was dead and is alive again; he was lost and is found." The parable ends with a hanging question: will the older brother come into the party? Will the older brother see the mercy of the father expressed to the younger son and choose to celebrate? Or will he remain outside, refusing to be a part of the family? This same question remained for the Jewish people in Paul's day as they responded to God's mercy to the Gentiles.

Reflection:

This passage demonstrates that no one is ever too far gone to be able to respond to the invitation to be a part of God's family. Is there someone that you know that you might think of as "too far gone" to be able to respond to the gospel?

_____

_____

Prayer Prompt:

Pray for the person that came to mind when you answered the reflection question. Ask that the Lord might give that person eyes to see, ears to hear, and a heart that is receptive to receive the gospel. And ask the Lord that you would be willing to be a part of that process if it is his will.

WEEK 9 - DAY 3

Scripture Reading - Romans 11:17-24

[17] If some of the branches have been broken off, and you, though a wild olive shoot, have been grafted in among the others and now share in the nourishing sap from the olive root, [18] do not consider yourself to be superior to those other branches. If you do, consider this: You do not support the root, but the root supports you. [19] You will say then, "Branches were broken off so that I could be grafted in." [20] Granted. But they were broken off because of unbelief, and you stand by faith. Do not be arrogant, but tremble. [21] For if God did not spare the natural branches, he will not spare you either.

[22] Consider therefore the kindness and sternness of God: sternness to those who fell, but kindness to you, provided that you continue in his kindness. Otherwise, you also will be cut off. [23] And if they do not persist in unbelief, they will be grafted in, for God is able to graft them in again. [24] After all, if you were cut out of an olive tree that is wild by nature, and contrary to nature were grafted into a cultivated olive tree, how much more readily will these, the natural branches, be grafted into their own olive tree!

Commentary:

Looking backward is a slow and frustrating thing. It feels inefficient and useless because the perception is, if you're not looking forward, you're not moving forward. However, as Paul explains the relationship between God and Israel, Paul asks the readers, particularly the Gentile (non-Jewish) readers, to consider the past in order to understand the present situation regarding the Gentiles being accepted into God's kingdom. Paul does this for two reasons:

First, Paul encourages the Gentiles in the Roman church to be grateful that they have been grafted into the family of God. While the Old Testament contains examples of non-Jewish people being brought into God's family (like Rahab and Ruth), the descendants of Abraham, Isaac, and Jacob were, and still are, the people that God originally intended to set apart for himself to make himself known to the nations (Genesis 12:2-3). He called them to live as humanity was intended to live, and to trust him in all things. However, in their attempts to do this, they fell short time and time again. Therefore, God, through Jesus, accomplished his purpose to extend salvation to all people, so that his chosen nation would eventually see the blessing they should have taken hold of, and turn back to him. As Paul puts it, Gentiles were "grafted in," like a branch that's joined to a vine it would never have naturally been part of. Therefore, the whole family of believers should be infinitely grateful, because without the love of God and his desire for all to be made right, we would be lost and enslaved by sin and death.

The second reason he takes a moment to look backward is to warn these Gentile believers in Rome. Paul knows the history of his own people, the Jewish people, and he knows how they grew ungrateful for their inheritance, driven by pride to find their own way apart from God. He also knows the same pride exists in every man and every woman, whether Jew or Gentile, and that the only defense against deceptive pride is holy humility.

No matter what side of the genealogical line we fall, Jew or Gentile, this passage serves as a poignant reminder that God deserves and demands our gratitude for who he is and the grace he's given and that should lead us to humility.

Reflection:

How can the relationship between God and Israel serve as a warning against pride and self-reliance in your own spiritual journey? What steps can you take to maintain a posture of gratitude and humility toward God?

_____

_____

How does the metaphor of being "grafted in" help you understand your connection to the larger narrative of God's plan?

_____

_____

Prayer Prompt:

Take a moment to thank God for the opportunity to be part of his Kingdom and pray for humility to remember that we didn't deserve it.

WEEK 9 - DAY 4

Scripture Reading: Romans 11:25-32

[25] I do not want you to be ignorant of this mystery, brothers and sisters, so that you may not be conceited: Israel has experienced a hardening in part until the full number of the Gentiles has come in, [26] and in this way all Israel will be saved. As it is written:

> "The deliverer will come from Zion;
> he will turn godlessness away from Jacob.
> [27] And this is my covenant with them
> when I take away their sins."

[28] As far as the gospel is concerned, they are enemies for your sake; but as far as election is concerned, they are loved on account of the patriarchs, [29] for God's gifts and his call are irrevocable. [30] Just as you who were at one time disobedient to God have now received mercy as a result of their disobedience, [31] so they too have now become disobedient in order that they too may now receive mercy as a result of God's mercy to you. [32] For God has bound everyone over to disobedience so that he may have mercy on them all.

Commentary:

One of life's most challenging moments arises when we grapple with the agonizing question, "Why, God?" Why, God, did you allow this? Why, God, didn't you stop that? Throughout human history, the purpose of suffering has perplexed the simple, the wise, and all in-between. For those in Christ, we may never know the specific reasons for the struggles we go through. However, we can trust that every tear-filled "Why, God?" can be answered by the truth that God is always in control and that the events of our lives are always for our good and His glory (Romans 8:28). Even more, one glorious day, he will wipe away every tear and He will make all things new (Revelation 21:5). After reconciling the eternal purposes God intends in our suffering, perhaps our most daunting question pivots from, "Why, God?," to "When, God?" When, God, will this struggle be over? When, God, will that be restored? Our "whys" long for divine purpose, and our "whens" beg for defined duration.

In today's passage, Paul answers a "Why, God?" question but only hints at a "When, God?" answer. Paul references a "mystery" about which he does not want his readers to be confused or "ignorant."

(11:25) What mystery was he referencing? Paul anticipates that Gentile believers in the Church of Rome might wonder "why" Israel, God's chosen people, had largely rejected Jesus and were not presently seeing the fulfillment of the Abrahamic covenant of Genesis 12. Paul explains that God purposed the disobedience of Israel to advance the Gospel among those outside of Israel. The Gospel message flowed from the Jewish Savior to Gentile hearts "as a result of their [Israel's] disobedience" (11:30). Paul highlights when "the full number of Gentiles has come in, Israel will be saved" (11:25) and "receive mercy." (11:31)

But what about "When, God?" When will Israel experience salvation by accepting Jesus as their deliverer? Paul's language conveys two possibilities of timing: one, a large-scale salvation of Jews, and two, "a steady, growing flow of Jews into Christianity."[1] But Paul also uses undefined words and phrases such as "until" (11:25), "will be" (11:25), "when" (11:27), and "now" (11:30, 31). In other words, the Holy Spirit, through the writings of Paul, confirms that God will be faithful to his promises to Israel but leaves the "When, God?" as a divine mystery.
Still today, God may whisper answers of purpose into our "Why, God?" questions, he may not fully resolve questions of timing when we plead to know when the suffering may pass. Lasting faith requires that we trust in the person and purposes of God, knowing that he has revealed his character, not his calendar.

Reflection:

What has God's Word shown us about his character that can build our trust in his calendar?

_____

_____

Prayer Prompt

Thank God that he is fully in control of the most perplexing and painful moments of your life. Ask him to reveal more about himself to you, through his Word, that you may experience abiding faith in every season of life.

WEEK 9 - DAY 5

Scripture Reading: Romans 11:33-36

[33] Oh, the depth of the riches of the wisdom and knowledge of God!
How unsearchable his judgments,
and his paths beyond tracing out!
[34] "Who has known the mind of the Lord?
Or who has been his counselor?"
[35] "Who has ever given to God,
that God should repay them?"
[36] For from him and through him and for him are all things.
To him be the glory forever! Amen.

Commentary:

In today's passage we come to the end of one of the most difficult and challenging portions of Scripture, Romans 9-11. In these three chapters, Paul has sought to address how God has been both sovereign and good in his dealings with the Jews and Gentiles throughout history. This topic was one that was deeply personal to Paul, and he wrote these chapters from a place of grieving over the state of his Jewish brothers and sisters in his day (Romans 9:2). After unpacking these difficult concepts, some of which remain a mystery (Romans 11:25), Paul takes a step back, and the only natural conclusion of this discussion for Paul is to praise God.

At the end of this weighty and heartfelt portion of Scripture, it's as though Paul looks up from his parchment and can't help but proclaim the righteousness and holiness of God. Paul has done his best to express in words the greatness and incomprehensible character of God. He is clearly overwhelmed by the character of God and the majesty of God's plan for salvation. He recognizes that God's ways and plans are beyond human understanding and he is left with the only proper response, worship.

After discussing mysteries and difficult truths, Paul writes, "Who has known the mind of the Lord? Or who has been his counselor?" This language echoes the analogy that Paul referenced in Romans 9 where God is the potter and we are simply the clay. Paul is saying that if anything within this past section of Scripture remains confusing, difficult to grasp, or hard to swallow, we must never forget that God is God and we are not. God's ways and thoughts are higher than our ways and our thoughts (Isaiah 55:8-9). Not only are we as humans not qualified to give God advice or counsel, but we have received from God far more than we deserve or could ever hope to repay.

Paul's final words in this section are a reminder that God is the one who made all things and all people, including Jews and Gentiles. He is the one who sustains all things, and he is the one who will receive all of the glory from his creation. In this paragraph, Paul joins in with all creation giving God the praise he infinitely deserves.

Reflection:

"God is God and we are not," is a helpful refrain to remind ourselves of frequently. How does that truth impact your day today?

_____

_____

What aspects of God's character can you praise him for today? Write a few of them down and stop and praise God for them.

_____

_____

Prayer Prompt:

In your prayer time today, repeat the words of our Scripture reading, Romans 11:33-36. Proclaim these words of praise to the Lord and meditate on the beautiful truths within this section of Scripture.

WEEK 10 - DAY 1

Scripture Reading - Romans 12:1-2

[1] Therefore, I urge you, brothers and sisters, in view of God's mercy, to offer your bodies as a living sacrifice, holy and pleasing to God—this is your true and proper worship. [2] Do not conform to the pattern of this world, but be transformed by the renewing of your mind. Then you will be able to test and approve what God's will is—his good, pleasing and perfect will.

Commentary:

Whenever we see the word "therefore" in Scripture, we have to ask what the "therefore" is "there for." Romans chapter 12 contains one of the most important "therefores" in all of Scripture. The first 11 chapters of Romans focus on Paul's theology and what a Christian should believe. In chapter 12, Paul begins to demonstrate for his readers how this theology directly impacts the way a believer should live. Paul's desire for the church in Rome is that their orthodoxy(right doctrine) aligns with their orthopraxy(right practice). Paul begins this section of his letter by calling the saints in Rome to be "living sacrifices." Paul knows that his readers would have been very familiar with the idea of animal sacrifices, but what does it mean to be a living sacrifice?

To be a living sacrifice means to live a life that is wholly and completely given to God. Paul expounds on this in verse 2. He says, "Do not conform to the pattern of this world." The world that we live in, whether we realize it or not, is perpetually shaping us. The world promotes certain beliefs and values that are in contradiction to the beliefs and values that a Christian is called to possess. Because this is all around us, it is the default way of living and thinking. However, followers of Christ are called to more. As living sacrifices, we are to reject and let die the ways and patterns of this world. Rather than conform, we are to "be transformed by the renewing of your mind." This means that we have to unlearn the world's ways, become like children, and learn the ways of Christ.

When we allow our minds to be renewed, everything changes. We begin to "love because he first loved us" (1 John 4:19). We learn to "in humility value others above ourselves" (Philippians 2:3). And we will be "able to test and approve what God's will is – his good, pleasing, and perfect will." The world wants us to follow their pattern, but God calls us to be living sacrifices, to lay ourselves down on the altar. But it is on that altar that life and life abundant is truly found.

Reflection:

What does Paul mean by "offer your bodies as a living sacrifice"?

_____

_____

Why does our minds need to be "renewed" in order to worship God and know his will?

_____

_____

Prayer Prompt:

Ask God to help you see his good, pleasing and perfect will. Ask him to help you offer your body, mind, and will to him in all ways as you strive to fulfill his will.

WEEK 10 - DAY 2

Scripture Reading - Romans 12:3-8

3 For by the grace given me I say to every one of you: Do not think of yourself more highly than you ought, but rather think of yourself with sober judgment, in accordance with the faith God has distributed to each of you. [4] For just as each of us has one body with many members, and these members do not all have the same function, [5] so in Christ we, though many, form one body, and each member belongs to all the others. [6] We have different gifts, according to the grace given to each of us. If your gift is prophesying, then prophesy in accordance with your faith; [7] if it is serving, then serve; if it is teaching, then teach; [8] if it is to encourage, then give encouragement; if it is giving, then give generously; if it is to lead, do it diligently; if it is to show mercy, do it cheerfully.

Commentary:

Paul talks in this section about the importance of how we as followers of Jesus are to live together as members of Christ's body, the Church. Throughout this letter, Paul addresses the relationship between Jewish believers and Gentile believers, and now Paul stresses the importance of unity within the family of God. The starting point of unity is humility, so Paul tells the church that they are not to think of themselves too highly, but rather they should look to the building up of others in the body of Christ.

Paul compares the community of believers to the human body in verses 4-5 to remind us that we're all members of one body. He encourages us to utilize our individual gifts for the benefit of the entire church. The total health and function of the body depends on the proper functioning of each individual part and the same is true with the different parts and people in the church. Each one of us who are believers have a gift (or gifts) to be used for the building up of the church and the strengthening of the other members of the church. We belong to each other, we minister to each other, and we need each other.

Paul says that each one of us have been given unique gifts and abilities that ought to be used within the body of Christ. We have the same standing in the gospel, but we are different in our varied abilities to minister to each other. All of us have been given distinct personalities, temperaments and gifts that equip us for a particular set of works that God has created us to do. Every good thing we have is only ours by

God's grace and intended to be used for his purpose. To fail to use God's gifts to serve each other is to fail to be a good steward.

Reflection:

What are the gifts that the Lord has given you?

_____

_____

How can you use your gifts to help build up your local church body?

_____

_____

Prayer Prompt:

Take a moment to thank God for the gifts he has given you. Ask him how you can use your gifts to help serve and build up your church family.

WEEK 10 - DAY 3

Scripture Reading - Romans 12:9-21

⁹ Love must be sincere. Hate what is evil; cling to what is good. ¹⁰ Be devoted to one another in love. Honor one another above yourselves. ¹¹ Never be lacking in zeal, but keep your spiritual fervor, serving the Lord. ¹² Be joyful in hope, patient in affliction, faithful in prayer. ¹³ Share with the Lord's people who are in need. Practice hospitality. ¹⁴ Bless those who persecute you; bless and do not curse. ¹⁵ Rejoice with those who rejoice; mourn with those who mourn. ¹⁶ Live in harmony with one another. Do not be proud, but be willing to associate with people of low position. Do not be conceited. ¹⁷ Do not repay anyone evil for evil. Be careful to do what is right in the eyes of everyone. ¹⁸ If it is possible, as far as it depends on you, live at peace with everyone. ¹⁹ Do not take revenge, my dear friends, but leave room for God's wrath, for it is written: "It is mine to avenge; I will repay," says the Lord. ²⁰ On the contrary: "If your enemy is hungry, feed him; if he is thirsty, give him something to drink. In doing this, you will heap burning coals on his head." ²¹ Do not be overcome by evil, but overcome evil with good.

Commentary:

Paul lays out in these verses some things that ought to characterize the life of all Christians. He's not giving us a to-do list to check off, but rather, these are things that are needed to make sure that the church is imitating Christ. Everything we do as followers of Christ must come from a heart of love. It must not be fake; it must be genuine, and believers must serve not only those in the church, but also those outside of the church.

Paul makes a bold statement at the beginning of verse 9 when he says, "Love must be sincere." Here, Paul is referring to an *agape* love - a love that remains steadfast even when circumstances change and even when your love is rejected. It is a love that mirrors the love that God has for all his children regardless of their actions and failures.

In verse 14, Paul echoes the words of Jesus during his Sermon on the Mount (Matthew 5:44). He says, "Bless those who persecute you; bless and do not curse." Paul shifts his focus from behavior within the Christian community to how Christians are to act toward those outside the church, even toward those who persecute it. Paul makes it clear that Christians are to love all people, even those who do not know or even reject Christ. While there are many evils in the world, Christians are to respond to those evils with love. We are called to be humble, forgiving and loving, just as Jesus was towards us.

Reflection:

What does Paul say our love toward others should be like? Do you feel you do this well?

In light of this passage, how do you respond towards people who are hard to love? In what ways do you need to change to better love your enemies?

Prayer Prompt:

Pray that God would open your eyes today for opportunities to show the love of Christ to someone this week. Pray for the Lord to soften your heart, even when it's hard.

WEEK 10 - DAY 4

Scripture Reading - Romans 13:1-7

¹ Let everyone be subject to the governing authorities, for there is no authority except that which God has established. The authorities that exist have been established by God. ² Consequently, whoever rebels against the authority is rebelling against what God has instituted, and those who do so will bring judgment on themselves. ³ For rulers hold no terror for those who do right, but for those who do wrong. Do you want to be free from fear of the one in authority? Then do what is right and you will be commended. ⁴ For the one in authority is God's servant for your good. But if you do wrong, be afraid, for rulers do not bear the sword for no reason. They are God's servants, agents of wrath to bring punishment on the wrongdoer. ⁵ Therefore, it is necessary to submit to the authorities, not only because of possible punishment but also as a matter of conscience. ⁶ This is also why you pay taxes, for the authorities are God's servants, who give their full time to governing. ⁷ Give to everyone what you owe them: If you owe taxes, pay taxes; if revenue, then revenue; if respect, then respect; if honor, then honor.

Commentary:

In these verses, Paul lays out how we as Christians should interact with the governing authorities that rule over us. Paul's goal here is to demonstrate that Christians should submit to their governing authorities, not because they are the ultimate authority of our life, but because God has instituted them in that position of authority over us.

Paul argues that active resistance against governmental authorities is actually a resistance to the ordinance of God and will result in judgment. Paul describes active resistance against authority as doing evil rather than good. He argues that it is necessary to submit ourselves to the authorities, not just because of the government's power to execute God's wrath, but also because we have a moral obligation as believers who have been made new in Christ Jesus. It is also noteworthy that Paul wrote these verses to a group of people that were living under the rule of the Roman Empire, a governing authority that was not aligned with Christian principles or values.

Looking at other portions of Scripture, we see that if the government were to make a decree that contradicted the decrees and character of God, then the Christian must obey God rather than man (Acts 5:29). But when the law is right and does not go against God's law, Christians must obey it if they hope to maintain a good conscience (1 Tim. 1:5, 19; 3:9; 4:2; Acts 24:16).

Lastly, in verse 7, Paul gives examples of how believers are to submit to the governing authorities by paying what we owe: taxes, revenue, respect, honor. If we do not, we show disrespect to the law, the officials, and ultimately the Lord.

Reflection:

What motivation do we as Christians have to submit to the government?

_____

_____

What does it look like as a believer in your culture to respect and honor the governing authorities?

_____

_____

Prayer Prompt:

Take a moment to pray for your local, state and national governmental leaders. Pray that the Lord will lead and guide them to make good, truthful and honorable decisions. Ask the Lord to work in your heart so that you can show respect and honor for those in leadership over you.

WEEK 10 - DAY 5

Scripture Reading - Romans 13:8-10

[8] Let no debt remain outstanding, except the continuing debt to love one another, for whoever loves others has fulfilled the law. [9] The commandments, "You shall not commit adultery," "You shall not murder," "You shall not steal," "You shall not covet," and whatever other command there may be, are summed up in this one command: "Love your neighbor as yourself." [10] Love does no harm to a neighbor. Therefore love is the fulfillment of the law.

Commentary:

In our previous passage, Paul spoke about paying the governmental authorities what is due to them. In the case of the government, we owe our obedience, as long as the government does not lead us to violate God's law and truth. Here, Paul continues to build off that same principle by talking about what is due to all people: love. "Love one another" is the basic principle of the Christian life. It is the "new commandment" that Christ gave to his disciples when he said "Love one another as I have loved you" (John 13:34).

Christians are to pay all their obligations, and there is one debt that we owe to all people. This debt to each other is not a financial one, but a debt of *love*. The debt we can never cease paying is the obligation we have to love one another. This obligation stems from the love that Christ demonstrated towards us (Romans 5:8). We are to continually view others as people who are owed our love. This love is owed to both those within the church and those outside of it and it should distinguish us from the rest of the world.

When we practice love, there is no need for any other laws, because love covers it all! If we love others, we will not sin against them. Paul then supports his claim that love fulfills the whole Law by referring to four commands from the Law that show us how we should relate to one another. He explains that these commands can be summarized in the single command to love our neighbors as ourselves. As believers, we do not live under the law, we live under grace. Our motivation for loving and serving others is the recognition of the same love that Christ showed us that we could never repay.

Reflection:

What are two practical ways you can pay the "debt of love" you owe to others this week?

_____

_____

Prayer Prompt:

Pray and ask God to give you a heart of love for all people in every circumstance. Ask him to help you love with the love that Christ has shown to you. Thank him for the example of love he showed us through his Son.

WEEK 11 - DAY 1

Scripture Reading - Romans 13:11-14

[11] And do this, understanding the present time: The hour has already come for you to wake up from your slumber, because our salvation is nearer now than when we first believed. [12] The night is nearly over; the day is almost here. So let us put aside the deeds of darkness and put on the armor of light. [13] Let us behave decently, as in the daytime, not in carousing and drunkenness, not in sexual immorality and debauchery, not in dissension and jealousy. [14] Rather, clothe yourselves with the Lord Jesus Christ, and do not think about how to gratify the desires of the flesh.

Commentary:

In our fast-paced world, it's easy to become spiritually complacent. These verses warn against this complacency and call believers to right living as we wait for Christ's return. Consider the lives of the following believers and how they "woke up," to right living:

A devoted church member named Deion has a long history of faith. Despite this, he has allowed work and social commitments to monopolize his schedule. He no longer takes time for spiritual things. However, reading verse 11, Deion realizes the urgency of rekindling his relationship with God. He starts setting aside time each morning for prayer and Bible study, awakening his spiritual fervor for the Lord.

Consider Sarah, a young woman struggling with negative influences and temptations in her social circle. Inspired by verse 12, she decides to make significant changes in her life. She distances herself from harmful environments and seeks out friendships that encourage her faith. By "putting on the armor of light," Sarah actively protects her spiritual well-being, embodying the virtues of Christ in her daily interactions.

Amir, a college student, finds himself caught up in the party scene, leading to behaviors that dishonor Christ. He's more popular than he's even been, but he doesn't feel like himself. After reading verse 13, he feels convicted to change his ways. He works instead to fill his schedule with social events that help him honor Christ - things like a guys' on-campus Bible study and local service projects. His new lifestyle, focused on devotion to the Lord and service to others, brings him peace and fulfillment, knowing he can stand before the Lord unashamed of his actions.

Gabriella is a businesswoman who is constantly chasing the next promotion and higher paycheck. She realizes that her pursuit of material gain has gradually overshadowed her spiritual values. Taking verse 14 to heart, Gabriella starts changing to reflect biblically ethical practice. She even starts mentoring young professionals, hoping to encourage a work culture that values others and not just "self." By "clothing herself with the Lord Jesus Christ," Gabriella realizes that she finds greater joy in serving others and aligning her professional life with her faith.

Romans 13:11-14 calls us to an active, Christ-centered life, urging us to wake from spiritual slumber, reject sinful behaviors, and embody Christ's virtues. Whether through personal devotion, being selective in who we spend time with, or integrating our faith into our professional life, these verses encourage us to live out our faith intentionally and authentically in today's world.

Reflection:

In what areas of your life have you become spiritually complacent or distracted?

What specific actions or behaviors in your daily life reflect the "armor of light" and the character of Jesus Christ? How can you more fully "clothe yourself with the Lord Jesus Christ" in your decisions, priorities, and social interactions?

Prayer Prompt:

Ask the Holy Spirit to reveal to you the areas of your life where you need to "clothe yourself with the Lord Jesus Christ."

WEEK 11 - DAY 2

Scripture Reading - Romans 14:1-4

¹ Accept the one whose faith is weak, without quarreling over disputable matters. ² One person's faith allows them to eat anything, but another, whose faith is weak, eats only vegetables. ³ The one who eats everything must not treat with contempt the one who does not, and the one who does not eat everything must not judge the one who does, for God has accepted them. ⁴ Who are you to judge someone else's servant? To their own master, servants stand or fall. And they will stand, for the Lord is able to make them stand.

Commentary:

Here Paul addresses the early Roman church, highlighting the importance of unity and acceptance among believers with differing convictions. He focuses on the principle of accepting those with "weak" faith without engaging in disputes over minor issues.

Paul uses dietary practices as an example. Some believers, likely with a background in Jewish dietary laws, abstained from certain foods, while others felt free to eat anything. For Paul, the primary concern is not related to the specific dietary laws but the attitude towards those with differing practices. Paul urges those who are "strong" in their faith not to look down on the "weak" and vice versa. He emphasizes that God has accepted both groups.

This passage underscores the necessity of humility and love within the Christian community. Judging others over disputable matters, which are not central to the faith, can lead to division and discord. Paul reminds us as believers that each of us is accountable to God alone. He alone is our master. We are no one's master, not even our own. We do well to remember that God's acceptance of all believers is what truly matters. We are all sinners in need of God's grace.

While accountability and discipleship are important aspects of our faith, and there are certainly occasions for church discipline, Jesus issued a harsh warning to anyone who thinks it their place to pass judgment on fellow believers. In Matthew 7:1-2, Jesus warned "Do not judge, or you too will be judged. For in the same way you judge others, you will be judged, and with the measure you use, it will be measured to you." Jesus calls us to have a spirit of grace and understanding towards others.

This passage encourages us to focus on what truly matters—our own growing relationship with Christ. While we are called to hold each other accountable as believers, we must do so having prayed over the situation and praying for the right spirit, for the right motivation, and for humility- acknowledging our own shortcomings and failures. Instead of arguing over minor differences in practices or opinions, we should strive to support and build each other up. This might mean showing respect for others' dietary choices, worship styles, or personal convictions, even if we feel justified in our own opinions. When we get this right, we create a church community where everyone feels welcomed and valued, reflecting the grace and acceptance of God. In daily interactions, let us practice patience, kindness, and understanding, remembering that our unity in Christ is more important than our differences.

Reflection:

Reflect on the thought that each person is ultimately accountable to God alone. How does this perspective influence the way you interact with and view other believers?

_____

_____

How do you react when you encounter fellow believers whose practices or convictions differ from you own?

_____

_____

Prayer Prompt:

Pray for unity and for peace in our churches. Ask God for wisdom and humility for any situations where loving correction and guidance might be necessary.

WEEK 11 - DAY 3

Scripture Reading - Romans 14:5-12

⁵ One person considers one day more sacred than another; another considers every day alike. Each of them should be fully convinced in their own mind. ⁶ Whoever regards one day as special does so to the Lord. Whoever eats meat does so to the Lord, for they give thanks to God; and whoever abstains does so to the Lord and gives thanks to God. ⁷ For none of us lives for ourselves alone, and none of us dies for ourselves alone. ⁸ If we live, we live for the Lord; and if we die, we die for the Lord. So, whether we live or die, we belong to the Lord. ⁹ For this very reason, Christ died and returned to life so that he might be the Lord of both the dead and the living.

¹⁰ You, then, why do you judge your brother or sister? Or why do you treat them with contempt? For we will all stand before God's judgment seat. ¹¹ It is written:

> "'As surely as I live,' says the Lord,
> 'every knee will bow before me;
> every tongue will acknowledge God.'"

¹² So then, each of us will give an account of ourselves to God.

Commentary:

Paul, in these verses, addresses the issue of personal convictions regarding sacred days and dietary practices. The central theme is the importance of honoring personal convictions while maintaining unity within the body of Christ. Paul emphasizes that whatever practices believers choose to follow, they should be done unto the Lord with gratitude and a clear conscience.

In today's multicultural and multi-denominational Christian environment, there are many different convictions about how to worship, how to dress, or what physical environment is most conducive to worship. Today, people subscribe to a variety of dietary restrictions for their health or for spiritual reasons. It's easy to judge, discredit, joke, or even ridicule those who don't eat certain foods or maintain certain spiritual practices. Paul reminds us that any practice, when done with a heart to honor God, should be respected.

Verses 7-8 remind us that our lives are not lived in isolation; our actions affect others in the community of faith. Whether we are young or old, living or dying, our life is to be lived for the glory of God. This means our daily actions and thoughts should reflect our devotion to Christ. Paul warns against judging others for their personal convictions. He calls for humility and grace. Each believer will give an account to God and it is not our place to judge others' motives, intentions, sincerity or devotion.

For example, imagine a Bible study where a heated debate breaks out about the appropriate way to dress for a church service. Some argue for formal attire, while others advocate for dressing casual. The debate goes back and forth until one of the older members speaks up. She has seen many trends come and go. She opens her Bible and begins to share from 1 Samuel 16:7, "The Lord does not look at the things people look at. People look at the outward appearance, but the Lord looks at the heart." Her words of wisdom from Scripture refocus the group's discussion to the posture of one's *heart* toward worship rather than anyone's outward appearance.

Romans 14:5-12 calls us to respect each other's personal convictions, live our lives unto the Lord, and avoid judgmental attitudes. By applying these principles, we can foster a more loving and unified Christian community. This passage encourages us to focus on our own accountability to God and to extend grace to others, recognizing that we are all on a journey of faith together.

Reflection:

Verse 12 reminds us that everyone will give an account to God. In light of this reality, what changes do you need to make in your life today to ensure that you are living in alignment with God's will and purpose for you?

Prayer Prompt:

Take time to think about how God has forgiven you, redeemed you, and given you a renewed purpose. Pray for a renewed spirit of peace, unity, conviction, and purpose in your life and in your circles of influence.

WEEK 11 - DAY 4

Scripture Reading - Romans 14:13-19

[13] Therefore let us stop passing judgment on one another. Instead, make up your mind not to put any stumbling block or obstacle in the way of a brother or sister. [14] I am convinced, being fully persuaded in the Lord Jesus, that nothing is unclean in itself. But if anyone regards something as unclean, then for that person it is unclean. [15] If your brother or sister is distressed because of what you eat, you are no longer acting in love. Do not by your eating destroy someone for whom Christ died. [16] Therefore do not let what you know is good be spoken of as evil. [17] For the kingdom of God is not a matter of eating and drinking, but of righteousness, peace and joy in the Holy Spirit, [18] because anyone who serves Christ in this way is pleasing to God and receives human approval.

[19] Let us therefore make every effort to do what leads to peace and to mutual edification.

Commentary:

The early Christian church in Rome was a melting pot of Jewish and Gentile believers. Jewish Christians had a heritage of dietary laws and religious customs from the Mosaic Law, while Gentile Christians came from various pagan backgrounds with no such restrictions. These cultural differences led to disputes in the church (see Acts 15 for an example of a dispute and how the early church resolved it). Paul wrote this portion of his letter to address these differences and to promote unity among the believers. While the church today doesn't deal with the same topics of dispute that the Jewish and Gentile Christians in Rome dealt with, the church today certainly does continue to struggle with disputes over matters of conviction and conscience. Paul urges the church in every age to prioritize love and mutual respect over personal convictions on disputable matters.

Paul urges us to show respect for others' beliefs and practices, especially in areas that are not central to the faith. He implores us to be mindful of how our behavior might be perceived by others, both within the church and in the community. We are Christ's ambassadors (2 Cor. 5:20) and we must strive to maintain a positive witness. As believers, we are called to live in a way that honors God and gains the respect of those around us, through acts of kindness, integrity, and peacemaking. Getting caught up in arguments and disagreements over disputable matters that are not essential to the faith robs us of the peace, joy and mutual respect that fosters unity in the church. Paul encourages the church to make every effort to build each other up in the faith. This approach not only honors God, but also creates a welcoming and supportive environment for all believers to grow in their walk with Christ.

Reflection:

Think about areas where your freedoms might inadvertently cause others to stumble. What steps can you take to ensure your actions are guided by love and consideration for others?

_____

_____

What specific actions can you take to build up and encourage others in your church or community? Are there conflicts that need resolution, relationships that need strengthening, or people that you have avoided that you need to reach out to?

_____

_____

Prayer Prompt:

Ask for forgiveness for when you may have inadvertently caused someone to stumble or for avoiding conflict or certain people. Ask God for the wisdom and courage to change your perspective, your heart, and your actions to better reflect that of our Lord and Savior, Jesus Christ.

WEEK 11 - DAY 5

Scripture Reading - Romans 14:20-23

[20] Do not destroy the work of God for the sake of food. All food is clean, but it is wrong for a person to eat anything that causes someone else to stumble. [21] It is better not to eat meat or drink wine or to do anything else that will cause your brother or sister to fall.

[22] So whatever you believe about these things keep between yourself and God. Blessed is the one who does not condemn himself by what he approves. [23] But whoever has doubts is condemned if they eat, because their eating is not from faith; and everything that does not come from faith is sin.

Commentary:

Romans 14:20-23 falls within a broader discussion in Romans 14 where Paul has been addressing the issue of Christian liberty. In particular, the discussion has been about how such freedoms, when exercised, have the potential for causing others to stumble. One of the biggest areas of contention in the church that Paul was writing to was over dietary laws. While the Jewish Christians viewed this as something important, necessary, and essential to their faith, Gentile Christians did not have the same conviction.

Paul reiterates that all food is clean (see Mark 7:19 and Acts 10:15), but acknowledges that causing another believer to stumble over food is destructive. The "work of God" Paul is referring to in verse 20 likely refers to the unity and edification of the church. The principle here: whether it is in regard to food, drink, or religious practices, our freedom should never come at the expense of another's spiritual well-being.

Paul also makes it clear that acting against one's conscience is sinful. If the Holy Spirit is convicting you about whether an action is right or wrong, and you proceed anyway, you are not acting out of faith. Faith, in this context, means a conviction that what you are doing is pleasing to God. Any action not rooted in this conviction is considered sin.

Lastly, Paul advises believers to keep their personal convictions about disputable matters between themselves and God. What is freedom to one person can mean chains for another. We do well not to flaunt our freedoms or advocate for them when those same freedoms can lead others to stumble.

Reflection:

How do you respond to others when they have different convictions than the ones you have, especially those that are biblical?

_____

_____

In what areas of your life do you need to be mindful of how your freedoms might impact others?

_____

_____

Prayer Prompt:

Pray for unity and peace in the church. Ask God for wisdom and discernment in exercising your freedoms. Ask God for a heart of love and sensitivity toward your brothers and sisters in Christ. And pray that the Holy Spirit would strengthen you with the resolve to follow God with integrity and humility.

WEEK 12 - DAY 1

Scripture Reading - Romans 15:1-13

¹ We who are strong ought to bear with the failings of the weak and not to please ourselves. ² Each of us should please our neighbors for their good, to build them up. ³ For even Christ did not please himself but, as it is written: "The insults of those who insult you have fallen on me." ⁴ For everything that was written in the past was written to teach us, so that through the endurance taught in the Scriptures and the encouragement they provide we might have hope. ⁵ May the God who gives endurance and encouragement give you the same attitude of mind toward each other that Christ Jesus had, ⁶ so that with one mind and one voice you may glorify the God and Father of our Lord Jesus Christ. ⁷ Accept one another, then, just as Christ accepted you, in order to bring praise to God. ⁸ For I tell you that Christ has become a servant of the Jews on behalf of God's truth, so that the promises made to the patriarchs might be confirmed ⁹ and, moreover, that the Gentiles might glorify God for his mercy. As it is written: "Therefore I will praise you among the Gentiles; I will sing the praises of your name." ¹⁰ Again, it says, "Rejoice, you Gentiles, with his people." ¹¹ And again, "Praise the Lord, all you Gentiles; let all the peoples extol him." ¹² And again, Isaiah says, "The Root of Jesse will spring up, one who will arise to rule over the nations; in him the Gentiles will hope." ¹³ May the God of hope fill you with all joy and peace as you trust in him, so that you may overflow with hope by the power of the Holy Spirit.

Commentary:

As Paul begins rounding out his letter, he broadens the scope from how believers should treat one another to how believers should treat everyone. He moves from writing about how we are to build up one another (fellow Christ-followers), to how we should be lifting up those who are simply "other," those that are not yet Christ-followers. Those "other" he calls our neighbors.

This concept of loving our neighbors is not unfamiliar in the realm of Judeo-Christian morality, but it's also not something that Christians have (at least publicly) maintained as a reputation. There's a reason for that- it's because it's hard and it's against our nature. Paul writes, "May the God who gives endurance and encouragement give you the same attitude of mind toward each other that Christ Jesus had, so that with one mind and one voice you may glorify the God and Father of our Lord Jesus Christ." Paul is telling us that, as believers we are to have one unified vision and mission- to lift Jesus high. This vision and mission drives us to love each other as believers, and also to love those around us for their good and God's glory. If this didn't take endurance and encouragement, we'd all be great at it, but it doesn't take long to look outside or in the mirror and realize it takes work.

Paul specifically uses the word, "endurance," for a reason. It's typically a word reserved for projects or long distance races or difficult health situations that require a lot of long-lasting, physical strength, but here Paul is applying it to relationships. In this, Paul calls us to a different kind of strength. It's the kind of strength that only comes from the Holy Spirit because it's not natural for us. It's the strength that joyfully bears with others. It's the kind of strength that displays the fruits of the Spirit that we don't usually enjoy exercising. It calls for patience and kindness and gentleness. It's the kind of strength that doesn't lead to trophies, but instead, it's the kind of strength that leads to unity among believers and leads to a contagious hope to those that aren't yet part of God's Kingdom, "...so that with one mind and one voice you may glorify the God and Father of our Lord Jesus Christ."

Reflection:

Why do you think Paul emphasizes endurance in the context of relationships? Can you identify a challenging relationship the Spirit is calling you to exercise this kind of love?

_____

_____

Prayer Prompt:

Pray for your heart to be molded in the likeness of Jesus' and for opportunities to glorify him in your relationships.

WEEK 12 - DAY 2

Scripture Reading - Romans 15:14-21

[14] I myself am convinced, my brothers and sisters, that you yourselves are full of goodness, filled with knowledge and competent to instruct one another. [15] Yet I have written you quite boldly on some points to remind you of them again, because of the grace God gave me [16] to be a minister of Christ Jesus to the Gentiles. He gave me the priestly duty of proclaiming the gospel of God, so that the Gentiles might become an offering acceptable to God, sanctified by the Holy Spirit. [17] Therefore I glory in Christ Jesus in my service to God. [18] I will not venture to speak of anything except what Christ has accomplished through me in leading the Gentiles to obey God by what I have said and done— [19] by the power of signs and wonders, through the power of the Spirit of God. So from Jerusalem all the way around to Illyricum, I have fully proclaimed the gospel of Christ. [20] It has always been my ambition to preach the gospel where Christ was not known, so that I would not be building on someone else's foundation. [21] Rather, as it is written: "Those who were not told about him will see, and those who have not heard will understand."

Commentary:

One of the most incredible things to realize is that the God who created the universe has given each one of us a purpose and a calling, and he equips us to fulfill that calling along the way. Paul continues in this portion of his letter by affirming the Roman church for what they've become. He encourages them by saying, "you yourselves are full of goodness, filled with knowledge and competent to instruct one another," meaning they're headed in the right direction, but Paul doesn't write a letter that's 16 chapters long just to say, "well done." He also writes to say, "we're not done yet!"

In the West, there's a general sense of how our rhythm of life should play out. We're born, we go to school, we work hard, and then slow down and coast as soon as we've done enough to afford a certain kind of lifestyle. Some might call it, "the American dream." In contrast to that sentiment, though, Paul is writing about where God has directed his life, and it only communicates one action, to lean in! He doesn't talk about how his season of sharing the Gospel will be slowing down or about how he *used to* preach to the Gentiles, no, he talks about what Christ has done through him and that he continues to "make it (his) ambition to preach the Gospel…" To Paul, this is not a season or a career, it's a calling.

When we consider God's purpose and calling for our lives, it's important that we don't confuse the trajectory of our work or school with the trajectory of our Kingdom work. When we graduate, our Kingdom work isn't over. When we retire, our Kingdom work isn't over, because this life is not all there is. So no matter our stage or age, we are to lean in to his purpose and his calling.

Reflection:

How does viewing your life as a continuous mission for the Kingdom differ from viewing it through the lens of a career or personal achievement?

_____

_____

In what ways can you "lean in" more to God's calling in your life, regardless of your age or stage?

_____

_____

Prayer Prompt:

Pray for an eternal perspective and supernatural energy to pursue God's calling to share the Gospel and grow more like him today and every day.

WEEK 12 - DAY 3

Scripture Reading - Romans 15:22-33

²² This is why I have often been hindered from coming to you. ²³ But now that there is no more place for me to work in these regions, and since I have been longing for many years to visit you, ²⁴ I plan to do so when I go to Spain. I hope to see you while passing through and to have you assist me on my journey there, after I have enjoyed your company for a while. ²⁵ Now, however, I am on my way to Jerusalem in the service of the Lord's people there. ²⁶ For Macedonia and Achaia were pleased to make a contribution for the poor among the Lord's people in Jerusalem. ²⁷ They were pleased to do it, and indeed they owe it to them. For if the Gentiles have shared in the Jews' spiritual blessings, they owe it to the Jews to share with them their material blessings. ²⁸ So after I have completed this task and have made sure that they have received this contribution, I will go to Spain and visit you on the way. ²⁹ I know that when I come to you, I will come in the full measure of the blessing of Christ. ³⁰ I urge you, brothers and sisters, by our Lord Jesus Christ and by the love of the Spirit, to join me in my struggle by praying to God for me. ³¹ Pray that I may be kept safe from the unbelievers in Judea and that the contribution I take to Jerusalem may be favorably received by the Lord's people there, ³² so that I may come to you with joy, by God's will, and in your company be refreshed. ³³ The God of peace be with you all. Amen.

Commentary:

Poverty and prayer go hand in hand, because desperation is the straightest path to dependence. When those things we lean on are stripped away, the only thing left is to lean on the Provider.

In what could be dismissed as Paul simply giving his travel plans, we have an insight into his priority list. First, he talks about his journey to Jerusalem. He's not visiting to start a church or because no one there has heard the Gospel, rather, it's because the church there is poor and needs the tangible help Paul is delivering. For someone so focused on evangelism, this seems like something he could delegate, but instead, he says the gifts provided by the Achaians and Macedonians were owed to the church in Jerusalem. In other words, this wasn't just a nice thing to do, it was his duty to his brothers and sisters in Christ to make sure they were taken care of spiritually *and* physically. This is still our responsibility for each other today, and in this passage Paul sees, acts, and receives both of these things.

Second, as Paul writes about the needs of the church in Jerusalem, he also turns and makes mention of his own needs. There are needs for safety and renewal as he travels, and in all of these things, he asks his brothers and sisters in Rome to join him. He asks them to partner in the struggle that awaits and for the travel ahead, to support him and lift him up. But there's a strange element to this request if we look around at the circumstances of this letter. If we match this up with Paul's travels, we'll realize he has never even visited this church. He asks that they would *join him* in his struggle by praying to the Lord for him, but he's spent zero time face to face with them. So how would they be able to join with him in an effective way? How would they be able to struggle alongside him?

The answer is prayer. The answer is to tap into this network that is the Kingdom of God, this family that can support and provide simply by calling upon the God that binds all believers together. In this passage we see the importance of our part in the community of believers. It is our part to give of what we physically have, and it's also our part to pray and lift up others for what only God can provide, whether near or far.

Reflection:

How does Paul's commitment to delivering aid to the church in Jerusalem, despite his focus on evangelism, challenge your understanding of the relationship between spiritual and practical support within the Christian community?

_____

_____

Prayer Prompt:

Pray for open eyes to see the physical needs that the Lord is asking you to meet. Pray also that God would open your heart to pray and join in the struggle with those serving him near and far.

WEEK 12 - DAY 4

Scripture Reading - Romans 16:1-16

¹ I commend to you our sister Phoebe, a deacon of the church in Cenchreae. ² I ask you to receive her in the Lord in a way worthy of his people and to give her any help she may need from you, for she has been the benefactor of many people, including me. ³ Greet Priscilla and Aquila, my co-workers in Christ Jesus. ⁴ They risked their lives for me. Not only I but all the churches of the Gentiles are grateful to them. ⁵ Greet also the church that meets at their house. Greet my dear friend Epenetus, who was the first convert to Christ in the province of Asia. ⁶ Greet Mary, who worked very hard for you. ⁷ Greet Andronicus and Junia, my fellow Jews who have been in prison with me. They are outstanding among the apostles, and they were in Christ before I was. ⁸ Greet Ampliatus, my dear friend in the Lord. ⁹ Greet Urbanus, our co-worker in Christ, and my dear friend Stachys. ¹⁰ Greet Apelles, whose fidelity to Christ has stood the test. Greet those who belong to the household of Aristobulus. ¹¹ Greet Herodion, my fellow Jew. Greet those in the household of Narcissus who are in the Lord. ¹² Greet Tryphena and Tryphosa, those women who work hard in the Lord. Greet my dear friend Persis, another woman who has worked very hard in the Lord. ¹³ Greet Rufus, chosen in the Lord, and his mother, who has been a mother to me, too. ¹⁴ Greet Asyncritus, Phlegon, Hermes, Patrobas, Hermas and the other brothers and sisters with them. ¹⁵ Greet Philologus, Julia, Nereus and his sister, and Olympas and all the Lord's people who are with them. ¹⁶ Greet one another with a holy kiss. All the churches of Christ send greetings.

Commentary:

At first, this passage seems like it would have little devotional value for us today. It is essentially a list of quick greetings and encouragements, like a head of state walking down a line shaking hands, or maybe, more accurately, the author's acknowledgements at the end of a book. They are rarely read or appreciated by anyone aside from those who have their names listed. But even in that, there is something to learn. From these verses we learn that people are important, and more specifically, an individual person is important. Paul would have had every reason to simply finish his letter with a general farewell, that reads something like, "you've all been a great help to me and to each other, I hope to see you soon." Instead though, he uses precious parchment space for a quick word to individuals.

Imagine we're in a small house, bumped up next to each other for lack of chairs or floor space. Children are darting in and around sweaty legs, while the adults hang on every word of the letter written from Paul, the father of churches all throughout Asia Minor. Each word feels like an epiphany and a conviction all at once, revealing the answers about this mysterious faith we're discovering together. And as the reader slows their cadence, the tone shifts. They read aloud a name and an encouragement. Then another name and their contribution. Some are whispering aloud how Paul even knew their name, and the tone shifts again when the one up front reads, "greet one another with a holy kiss. All the churches of Christ greet you."

How impactful would that moment have been? Whether their specific name was mentioned or not, there would have been an instant sense that we're all in this together. This isn't a far off movement or an abandoned, isolated group, this is a family separated by geography, but bonded by their spiritual inheritance. This is a royal priesthood of which we get to take part.

Paul understands the significance of giving this news to the masses, but also that the Gospel he preaches is for each man and each woman. It's for every heart and every mind, by name. Two thousand-plus years later, this truth is still the same, and in a way Paul could never do, Jesus still knows us and calls us- every man and every woman-by name.

Reflection:

Why might it be significant that Paul takes time to acknowledge specific people and their contributions rather than offering a generic farewell? How does this approach reflect the value of each person's role in the body of Christ?

_____

_____

Prayer Prompt:

Make a list of those in your life that the Lord has used to encourage you in your faith and walk. Take a moment to thank God for each of them by name and to pray for them.

WEEK 12 - DAY 5

Scripture Reading - Romans 16:17-27

[17] I urge you, brothers and sisters, to watch out for those who cause divisions and put obstacles in your way that are contrary to the teaching you have learned. Keep away from them. [18] For such people are not serving our Lord Christ, but their own appetites. By smooth talk and flattery they deceive the minds of naive people. [19] Everyone has heard about your obedience, so I rejoice because of you; but I want you to be wise about what is good, and innocent about what is evil. [20] The God of peace will soon crush Satan under your feet. The grace of our Lord Jesus be with you. [21] Timothy, my co-worker, sends his greetings to you, as do Lucius, Jason and Sosipater, my fellow Jews. [22] I, Tertius, who wrote down this letter, greet you in the Lord. [23] Gaius, whose hospitality I and the whole church here enjoy, sends you his greetings. Erastus, who is the city's director of public works, and our brother Quartus send you their greetings. [25] Now to him who is able to establish you in accordance with my gospel, the message I proclaim about Jesus Christ, in keeping with the revelation of the mystery hidden for long ages past, [26] but now revealed and made known through the prophetic writings by the command of the eternal God, so that all the Gentiles might come to the obedience that comes from faith— [27] to the only wise God be glory forever through Jesus Christ! Amen.

Commentary:

Love. Salvation. Power.

The significance of the Gospel can't be overstated. It is the good news that God loved and loves us in spite of our rebellion. He loves us so much, in fact, that he provides salvation to all who believe, through his son who experienced the death we all deserve. And in so doing, he also grants us power through his Spirit as part of our inheritance.

This is the Gospel that Paul points toward throughout this entire letter. In chapters 1-5, he walks through how we have been made right before God and, "obtained access by faith into this grace in which we stand " (5:2), and then chapters 6-8 and 12-15, how we have no other response but to be transformed into reflections of him in what we say and do. And finally we come to the end of this letter. Paul implores these house churches in Rome (and us) to cement these truths in their hearts and guard against anyone who would try to add or take away from this beautiful, simple Gospel. God displayed love through the salvation of his son and gave power through the Holy Spirit to all who believe. There is nothing more or less to be added, and anyone that would suggest otherwise is doing nothing more than leading away from the truth of Jesus.

As we come to the end of our study through Paul's letter to the Romans, let us faithfully carry the baton our spiritual mothers and fathers have passed to us. Let us faithfully live in the *love* of the Father, the *salvation* of the Son and the *power* of the Holy Spirit.

Reflection:

Why is it important to recognize and resist influences that distort the Gospel? And, according to verses 17-18, how can you identify those influences?

_____

_____

Take a moment to reflect on the love of the Father, the salvation through the Son, and the power of the Holy Spirit. In a tangible, practical way, how can you live out these truths today?

_____

_____

Prayer Prompt:

Pray for a greater understanding of the love God has for us and for the Spirit to reveal how we can better reflect him today, tomorrow and the days to follow.

Made in the USA
Columbia, SC
15 October 2024

44435999R00068